Terrorism, Islam, and Christian Hope

Reflections on 9-11
and Resurging Islam

Terrorism, Islam, and Christian Hope
Reflections on 9-11 and Resurging Islam

James B. De Young

Resource Publications
An imprint of Wipf and Stock Publishers
Eugene, Oregon

Resource Publications
An imprint of Wipf and Stock Publishers
199 West 8th Avenue, Suite 3
Eugene, OR 97401

Terrorism, Islam, and Christian Hope
Reflections on 9-11 and Resurging Islam
Copyright©2004 by James B. De Young
ISBN: 1-59752-005-5
Publication Date: December 2004

TABLE OF CONTENTS

INTRODUCTION

The following pages represent two broad areas of concern and two different ways to address them. Therefore, the book is divided into two parts to reflect these different concerns. In the first part, I express the impact that the events of September 11, 2001, have had on me, and, I assume, on other Christians. These reflections are numbered and dated as they were written, journaling the events and their meaning as they unfolded. I seek to understand what these events reflect from the past, what they mean now, and what they portend for the future. Should they awaken in us concerns that we have not felt before—concerns for safety, security, direction as a nation? Do Christians have something special at stake? Do they reflect a failure to take seriously the rise and influence of Islam? Do they reflect a certain smugness about our own Christian values and mission that has left us in a stupor, of sorts, instead of vigorously pursuing a case for them in the public square? Do the events of 9-11 parallel past climatic times when Islam and Christianity came into conflict? Are we in such a conflict now? More importantly, what can Christians do to renew the Christian quest for the kingdom of God? I also include reflections of my visit to the U.A.E. and Afghanistan in the summer of 2003.

In the second part, I more directly address the resurgence of Islam occurring throughout the world. For over sixteen centuries Islam has been the most formidable opponent to Christianity. In part this results from its manifest rise after the coming of Judaism and Christianity, and its claim to be a successor to both and to be supreme to both. Yet in modern times, the bold challenge of extremist Islam to the "Christian West," with the stated goal of bringing the latter to its knees, reinforces the image of its aggressive posture. Its resurgence in numbers and influence is clear.

In this second part I suggest that the resurgence of Islam is the result of at least three important forces. First, Islam employs the historical-critical method, a skeptical approach to the Bible, that so-called Christians themselves have used to undermine an orthodox, evangelical view of Christianity. Islam seizes upon the work of these Christians in their negative interpretation of the central doctrines of Christianity (the deity of Christ, his miracles, his atoning death, his resurrection, the reality of sin) in order to convince Christians that Islam has the only correct interpretation of the life of Christ.

The second force contributing to the resurgence of Islam is the growing secular mindset in the West including the United States. This secularism contributes to the first factor. To the extent that we become increasingly secular or naturalistic in our view of reality we become susceptible to a negative or secular interpretation of Scripture. We are less willing to make commitment to truth, to spiritual values, to the unseen world, and to a godly, moral life.

The third force contributing to the resurgence of Islam is globalization. The increasing ability for everyone, including the followers of Islam, to spread ideas, goods, language, culture, and religion around the world makes Islam almost instantly accessible to all. The failure of sociologists to recognize the role of religion in globalization is a serious matter and discussed in this section.

In the first part of the book I present my own musings and reflections on the events of 9-11. In the second half I present my response to a Muslim-authored book written to convince Christians to convert to Islam. I cite various written sources to substantiate my concerns. This book attacks Christian beliefs from the viewpoint of Islam, and I seek to refute it point-by-point, both with my own insights based on Scripture and those of others.

In the appendices I briefly address the Muslim mindset toward Christianity; I critique the historical-critical method; I compare Jesus and Muhammad; and I contrast the Allah of the Qur'an with the God of the Bible.

Today a Crescent Curtain looms over civilization. It threatens to bring a darkness on civilization unseen in the past two thousand years. All the good that the light of Christianity has fostered will be clouded, blighted, even extinguished.

My desire is that this work will contribute both to a greater understanding of the differences between Christianity and Islam, and to a renewal of evangelical faith and commitment. It is only the latter that is able to meet the resurging challenge of the crescent to the cross.

PART ONE

REFLECTIONS ON 9-11

#1
REFLECTIONS ON GRIEVING
AT A TIME OF NATIONAL DISASTER
Some Initial Thoughts
Sept. 13, 2001

The tragic events that wrecked our nation's sense of repose on September 11, 2001, have brought to many a sense of almost unbearable grief. I find myself among them. As I listen and watch the unrelenting news of the horror that struck the World Trade Center and the Pentagon the sense of grief wells up within me. The reports of thousands of people losing their lives in an almost unbelievable horror of explosion and fire, of people leaping to their deaths from heights of 1000 feet, bring repeated tears. When I've thought that the news could no longer so move me something else reinforces the terrible suffering and I find myself weeping again.

I've thought frequently why I find myself given to tears. Why do I weep? What is it that deeply moves us all at this tragic time in our country's experience? Perhaps putting my thoughts on paper will help me understand, and perhaps bring fuller understanding to us all.

Weeping is a way to identify with those who have sustained such unbelievable suffering and horrible death. It is a sign that I belong to a community that extends to millions of people, yet these are my friends and neighbors. It matters not that they were personally unknown to me. They are fellow-citizens of a large nation, common people for the most part. I realize that they were totally unsuspecting that their lives were going to end on Tuesday, and I realize how fragile my life is on any given day.

I find myself weeping because I want those who have suffered and those who have died to know that I care, that I am equally vulnerable, that there is a humbling sense that "this could have happened to me." What happened to them happened to all of us. I want to join them to assert that I am equally affected by my own weak humanity, that I too have questions: Why should this happen? Why would God allow this? How could fellow human beings engage in such despicable evil toward others, innocent bystanders to larger conflict in the world? Why is there such evil in the world?

Weeping arises as I reflect on the fact that many of those who died passed into a Christless eternity. All opportunity to make peace with God has passed. How many were lost? How many, perhaps just before their death, reached out for God in their last moments? How many came to faith and so passed from death to life even as their physical lives abruptly ended?

I weep because at such a tragedy as this there is, at least for a brief time, an almost universal affirmation that there are ultimate values that transcend our material ones. At times like these we come to recognize the power of prayer; we affirm the need for hope, faith, even peace with God. We affirm that we are all the offspring of God (Acts 17:29). We affirm a reality that transcends what we can see and hear. I weep because I sense that we do not give enough attention to these values in the "ordinary" course of our living. It is sad to realize that we should ever think that we could neglect these values until such times as these. It is heartbreaking to realize that we live so much of our lives without a concern for God and his kingdom, that we choose to suffer the loss of his presence, comfort, peace, and strength.

So I weep because God weeps. Being made in his image and likeness means that my feelings reflect the feelings, the tears and the joy, of God. When I suffer God cares. The Almighty One himself chooses not to reverse the choices we make to live without him, to deny him, and he grieves. The Old Testament prophets themselves were inspired to reflect in similar ways. When Israel and Judah had gone far in sin, Jeremiah recorded God as exclaiming: "Oh, that my head were waters, and my eyes a fountain of tears, that I might weep day and night for the slain of the daughter of my people!" (Jer. 9:1; cf. v. 10). Lest we think that it is unfitting for the

Almighty to weep, that he should ever have a need to do so, the truth is that it is just because he is Almighty that he is able to weep. His weeping displays that he is not only transcendent but also immanent. He knows his own identity as no other being in the universe does; his identity is within himself. He is not threatened by the reality of others as separate persons or by anything in the universe. Because he both knows and assures the final accomplishment of his will, he is able to attend to each individual. He is the only one able to attend perfectly to the reality of all of us.

We can never overstate the place of love in our weeping. Love is the greatest force in the universe. It is love that lies behind our compassion and expressions of caring. It is love that not only led God to choose the finality he desires but secures it. God is love, and since we are made in his image and likeness, God's plans will be realized through people redeemed by love as they choose love. It is love which lies behind our tears and grief, just as it lies behind God's.

I weep because Jesus wept. If there should be any doubt that God cares so much as to weep, Jesus settles all doubts. Because Jesus knew his identity, he was able to pay attention to others. Indeed, he identified himself with us in our human condition more fully than any other human ever could. He suffered as no one else, and he wept. When his close friend Lazarus died, Jesus stood at his tomb and wept (John 11:1-44). His weeping was not because he missed Lazarus or because of similar reasons, but because he looked at the others gathered around, weeping from their sense of loss. He entered into their experience, their sense of loss; he identified with them.

On another occasion Jesus wept over the hardness of the human heart that refused to embrace his offer of redemption and forgiveness, that rejected his peace. It was his own people who rejected him (Luke 13:34; 19:41-42).

The experience of the thousands who died on September 11 is our experience. We learn from Jesus that it is only those who know their identity who have the strength to attend to the reality of others, to enter into their experience, and feel what they feel. We become like Jesus by growing in our identity with him, in our relationship, with him. We develop the mind of Christ. In doing this we come to possess the strength and serenity that comes from our loving, all-knowing, all-powerful God. We are released from self-centeredness and fear, and liberated to attend to the reality of others. We also learn how to attend to the reality of God, to engage in mutual interpersonal relationship. And God comes to experience us in newer ways as we relate to him.

Jesus himself gave specific attention to those who are overwhelmed with grief and suffering. Indeed, his kingdom is especially oriented toward such. In the beatitudes, he said that the truly happy people in the kingdom are those who suffer and mourn, for they will know the special comfort of God himself. They are the special object of his concern and love (Matt. 5:4). Why else should God care unless our suffering deeply moves him?

A final word about sorrow and weeping. For the Christian there is the hope, the assurance, of a resurrection to an inexpressibly delightful future. We sorrow not as those who have no hope, who have only despair and a bleak future. Thus Paul exhorted believers to comfort one another with this hope (1 Thess. 4:13-18).

The Psalmist captured the twofold anchor of the believer's stability— the strength and love of God. Even in the time of severe testing, God is sufficient for all our need.

"One thing God has spoken,
Two things have I heard;
That you, O God, are strong,
And that you, O Lord, are loving." Psalm 62:11-12

"When my heart was grieved
and my spirit embittered,
I was senseless and ignorant;
I was a brute beast before you.
Yet I am always with you;
you hold me by my right hand.
You guide me with your counsel,
and afterward you will take me into glory.
Whom have I in heaven but you?

And earth has nothing I desire besides you.
My flesh and my heart may fail,
but God is the strength of my heart
and my portion forever." Psalm 73:21-26.

#2
"WE HAVE EVERYTHING TO FEAR, INCLUDING FEAR ITSELF"
Some Reflections On the Motivation for the Recent Terrorist Attacks On the United States
September 14, 2001

As long as we as a nation treat the terrorist tragedy in New York City and Washington D. C. as simply a military or political struggle we are doomed to misunderstand our enemy and to compromise our ability to respond successfully.

In 1996 Osama Bin Laden declared a holy war, a jihad, on the United States. A couple years later he issued a *fatwa*, a religious ruling, that calls for the killing of Americans, civilian and military, in any country where they may be. If current intelligence efforts confirm Bin Laden as the source or the inspirer of those who killed about 3000 innocent people by their suicidal acts, then we are dealing with a formidable enemy.

He is not formidable because of his financial or military strength, or his numbers, for he is inferior to our nation's resources for these. His strength lies in his Islamic fundamentalism and his terrorist tactics. He views the United States as the great Satan, as the evil purveyor of oppression, exploitation, and desecrator of the world community. He views us as evil because we export around the world indecency, irreligion, and corruption. His motivation is religious, perverted though it may be. He uses religion to fuel anti-American sentiment around the world.

Islamic fundamentalism seeks to extend the rule of the Qur'an throughout society by forcing *sharia* as the law of the land. The worship of Allah by standards expressed in the Qur'an would alone prevail. Islam would control all institutions and the entire way of life. Religion, economics, education, government, the courts, the arts, the media, entertainment—everything would come under the control of a small, elite class of religious zealots who judge themselves as the only ones capable of interpreting the Qur'an for application to daily life.

Little, if any, place would be given to other views, other faiths, other cultural expressions. This way of life would be forced upon the majority. Anarchy and rebellion on behalf of this brand of Islam is accepted, even glorified. It is the religious promise of Islamic fundamentalism that makes the terrorists willing to commit suicide in their attempts to destroy us. As martyrs they secure instant paradise.

The events of September 11 represent, at the core, a conflict of one set of spiritual values against another. It constitutes a danger for the twenty-first century more serious than that posed by communism in the twentieth century. As President Bush said, it is the first war of the twenty-first century.

America's values of freedom and respect for the dignity of every human being as made in the image of God, of respect for duly constituted authority, of equal justice before the law all derive from a spiritual heritage that ultimately goes back to the Bible. Our toleration of diversity, of freedom of expression, of the press, of assembly, of religion are all anchored in spiritual values and principles that come from our Creator. These values have made us the most successful nation of modern times. Bin Laden knows this.

Yet Bin Laden also knows that for decades we have slandered, vilified, and rejected these spiritual values in our daily life, in our institutions, in our media—the very values that laid the foundation for our greatness. Bin Laden and terrorists like him believe that we have become vulnerable to attack and to the success of those attacks because we have become weak in the area of morality and spiritual values.

Unfortunately, the indictment of the United States is all too true. We need only look at the evidence of our corruption. In many respects we have become the world's greatest purveyor of immorality and violence via the media, the world's greatest consumer of drugs and alcohol. Our wealth has made us materialistic, a culture seeking instant gratification via goods, entertainment, and sport. While church attendance is still at a level higher than in any other country of the West, the impact of spiritual values on our culture has steadily declined. Even among the people of our churches there are epidemics of pornography, divorce and broken homes, and abortion. This erosion of our values makes us an undisciplined, vulnerable nation.

More recently Bin Laden declared that America is not as strong as she appears. The terrorism of September 11 suggests that he is correct to a degree neither he nor we could have imagined just a few days before. Just a few evil men were able to kill thousands of people, destroy the greatest trade center in the world, affect financial markets world wide and foster universal financial uncertainty, shut down for the first time in history the entire airline industry, and permanently scar our national psyche.

For a thousand years until the 1700's Islam was a predominant force in the world. In the twelfth century it succeeded in defeating Christian Europe in its attempts to claim the Holy Land. Once again, if the West fails to address and reassert its spiritual values, we have every reason to fear that Islamic fundamentalists will incite millions of followers and assume political control in many countries. They will succeed, if not in destroying our country, then in terrorizing it in protracted conflict for decades to come. Historians may one day look back on the events of September 11, 2001, as marking the beginning of the beginning for a resurgence of militant Islam rather than the beginning of the end for the anarchy it has fostered.

These words do not seek to indict Islam per se, particularly with respect to the recent terrorism. The terrorists represent a small segment of Islam and a perverse interpretation of the Qur'an. Mainstream Islamic scholars view Bin Laden "as a religious pretender with no credentials as a Muslim cleric."[1] He has had no formal theological training. A *fatwa* can only be authoritative if issued by a recognized Muslim cleric or highly respected Islamic scholar.[2] Most Muslims view his radical and violent ideology as opposed to the teachings of the Qur'an and traditional Islamic doctrine. Yet Bin Laden has obtained the endorsement of leading extremist Islamic clerics. While scholars may reject his credentials, the vast impoverished millions of Islamic youth could care little about what scholars think as

[1] Jeffery L. Sheler, "Of faith, fear, and fanatics," *USNWR* (Sept. 24, 2001) 56.
[2] Ibid.

long as he embraces Islamic fundamentalism and uses it to validate his political ambitions.

Indeed, many moderate Islamic nations in Central Asia have more to fear than we do. Their people are considered to be hypocrites, worthy of death (*Qur'an,* Surah, 30:60). The Taliban and other radical groups have sent missionaries to Central Asia to work among the many unemployed young men and turn them into terrorists.

Will and Ariel Durant spent much of their lives searching for the basic elements of what constituted a civilized society during the past two thousand years. In *The Story of Civilization,* they concluded that four elements were necessary for civilization: a system of government, a system of economics, education and the arts, and public morality. Even though they were agnostics they also discovered that public morality could not exist without religion. The recent collapse of communism gives amazing validation to their conclusion.

There is precedent for an inferior force conquering a wealthier, mightier nation. In the fifth century, Rome was sacked by barbarians because her wealth and immorality had made her weak and vulnerable.

The application of the study by the Durants to the present struggle is clear. At our peril we neglect the spiritual and moral dimensions of this struggle.

The need for a public discussion of the moral and spiritual inferiority of Islamic fundamentalism needs to occur, for our own benefit and for the world's. After all, Christians are not terrorizing the world today and justifying it in the name of Christ. They are not engaged in the murder of hundreds and thousands of innocent civilians in the name of religion.

The values of Islam need to be examined in light of the words of Christ regarding the nature of his kingdom and its foundational, core value of love. The pertinent question for us today is: What kind of actions do these values foster?

This question has a clear answer for the followers of Christ. He calls us to forgive our enemies. He himself lived out these words in his personal example. It violates the ethics of Christianity to seek out for harm or persecution those who are Muslim, or any other individual for that matter. While the State bears the sword to secure justice (Romans 13:1-6), the individual is compelled by love to follow the example of Christ.

We need a spiritual renewal, a revival, of biblical faith that will reform our institutions and our culture. Only Christians as salt and light, Jesus said, can make the world work (Matt. 5:13-16). Only those, whether Christian or not, who embrace these values can change the world for good.

When President Roosevelt called America out of the Great Depression, he affirmed that the only thing we had to fear was fear itself. Such despoiling of fear and panic arises out of a people's moral and spiritual strength. But when these foundations are gone, everything becomes a reason to fear including fear itself.

The Psalmist of old recognized that fear was a basic condition that terrorized people. In the face of seemingly insurmountable obstacles he pointed to the defeat of fear by spiritual realities. He wrote:

"God is our refuge and strength, an ever present help in trouble. Therefore we will not fear, though the earth give way and the mountains fall into the sea, though its waters roar and foam and the mountains quake with their surging." (Psalm 46:1-2).

The Psalmist also recognized that strength is found in God, not in military might nor numbers. Fearing God will deliver from all other fears.

"The LORD foils the plans of the nations; he thwarts the purposes of the peoples.
But the plans of the LORD stand firm forever, the purposes of his heart through all generations.
Blessed is the nation whose God is the LORD, the people he chose for his inheritance. . . .
No king is saved by the size of his army; no warrior escapes by his great strength.
A horse is a vain hope for deliverance; despite all its great strength it cannot save.
But the eyes of the LORD are on those who fear him, on those whose hope is in his unfailing love, to deliver them from death and keep them alive in famine." Psalm 33:10-12, 16-19.

#3
FROM TOURS TO AMERICA
What Does the Battle of Tours Have in Common with the
Recent Terrorist Attacks On the United States?
September 26, 2001

Islam was "born" in the year 622 when Mohammed fled from Mecca to Medina in what is now Saudi Arabia. By the time of Mohammed's death in 632 Islam had captured all of Arabia. Within one hundred years it had taken from Christianity most of North Africa, Syria, Palestine, Egypt, and Persia. In 637 the Mosque of Omar was built in Jerusalem, and still stands there as the Dome of the Rock. Islam was halted in the East by Leo the Isaurian in 717 and 718. After overrunning Spain Islam was stopped in the West by the Franks under Charles Martel near Tours (now France) in 732. If Martel had not halted Islam at that point it is likely that it would have taken all of Western Europe.

Later, the Crusades sought to reclaim the Holy Land for Christianity (it had held Israel from the 4th century till the conquest by Islam). From 1071 onward the fanatical and brutal Seljuk Turks had taken much of Asia Minor and had replaced the more placid Arabs in their hold on Palestine. The Turks made pilgrimages to Jerusalem almost impossible and desecrated the holy places. Islam was also threatening the Eastern empire under Alexius the Christian emperor at Constantinople. In 1099 the First Crusade succeeded in taking Jerusalem. But the Muslims under Saladin retook it in 1187—less than a hundred years later—and have held it until just a few years ago (there was a brief time from 1229 to 1244 when the Christians held Jerusalem before the Saracens reclaimed it for

Islam). Only in 1948 has Israel emerged as a free state not dominated by Islam or Christianity. The only foreign religion trying to dominate Israel today is Islam, once again.

Islam remained a major force in the world until the late 1600's when the Ottoman Turks sought to subjugate all of Europe. They conquered Greece, Yugoslavia, Bulgaria, part of Romania, and most of Hungary. Only outside the walls of Vienna, Austria, were they halted in the year 1683. The city's 20,000 defenders resisted a Muslim army of 300,000 men.

While not always intolerant, Islam far too often offered conquered peoples only three options: the sword, tribute or Islam. If Islam had conquered Western Europe in the 8th century, or again in the 17th century, it is doubtful that the modern world as we know it would look much like it does today, with the United States leading the way in democracy and freedom.

The reason for rehearsing this bit of history is to point to parallels, as I see them, between the 8th century and today. In recent decades Islam has been inflamed by extremists who desire to conquer once again, in the name of Allah, lands they once held, and new lands never held, such as the United States and Western Europe. Radical Islam has expanded across Central Asia, in Egypt and North Africa, East Africa and Nigeria, and across India and the vast islands of Indonesia. This onward march of Islamic fundamentalism is as equally merciless today as was the Islam of the 7th and 8th centuries.

Times have changed, ideologies have come and gone, independent nations have emerged, and the world is much different today from what it was 1300 years ago. Yet fundamentalist Islam has not changed; it has only lain dormant for this long time.

Why has Islamic extremism raised its ugly, crusading head again? The reasons are many, but perhaps there are two or three main ones. The first would be the growing wealth and prosperity of the West and the growing impoverishment of Muslim lands. This has bred a sense of hostility because the Muslim peoples believe that the wealth of the West has come at their expense and threatens their culture. There is also the spread of Western technology that enables even impoverished peoples, even when in the minority, to possess modern weapons, even weapons of mass destruction, to cower others into submission, as the Taliban have done in Afghanistan, as Saddam Hussein has done to the Kurds in Iraq.

But the major reason must be recognized as religious. Islam has never totally disavowed the use of force in the name of Allah. Even after the events of Terrible Tuesday, the number of Islamic clerics swearing off all violence are too few. It has never embraced the highest ethic of all—love, the watchword of the kingdom of Christ. Being fatalistic and justifying the means by the end—the glory of Allah—people can be forced into submission. Freedom of religion, basic to all other freedoms, has not followed in the tracks of Islam as it has followed in the tracks of Christianity. Instead totalitarianism and oppression are the trademarks of Islamic fundamentalism.

The conflict is ultimately a spiritual or religious one. The Old Testament is sacred to Jews, Christians, and Muslims. Yet only one of these religions—Islam in its extremist form—seeks to advance itself today by murder, mayhem, and anarchy on a global scale. Christianity and Judaism are not involved in terrorism to expand their borders. In its oppressive program Islamic fundamentalism stands self-condemned. As President Bush so eloquently said (in his address to the nation and to the world on September 20, 2001), "those who do evil in the name of Allah blaspheme the name of Allah." We are not deceived, the President said, by "their pretenses to piety."

Let's be clear what the core of the current conflict is. It is essentially not so much between Islam and the West, but Islam versus Islam. It is between extremist Islam and traditional Islam. As President Bush also said: "The terrorists are traitors to their own faith, trying, in effect, to hijack Islam itself." The nations of the West must help traditional Islam to succeed in the theological struggle within Islam, or we may indeed face, in the words of Jay Tolson, a "real and possibly cataclysmic clash between civilizations" (in his sober article, "Fight to the Finish: Has a 'Clash of Civilizations' threatened the 'end of history'?" *USNWR* [Oct. 1, 2001], 39).

Only a robust faith will provide those values and spiritual strength necessary to a patriotism that will take us through a prolonged conflict. To avoid defeat or an impasse, we are in need of a spiritual renewal. We have exported our sins as much as our technology. We have much evil to confess, much wickedness to forsake. Hollywood and the media should lead the way. No matter how often we may intone, "God bless America," we will be as guilty of "pretenses to piety" as the terrorists are.

An oppressive Crescent Curtain is expanding to enclose formerly moderate Islamic lands within its domain. The numbers of radicalized Muslim youths are growing by the millions. Radicalized Islam boasts a history of almost 1400 years, and promises a good life now and paradise in the life to come (and a harem of 72 for every martyr!). Where will it lead in the 21st century? What new social orders will emerge? How can it be stopped? No one can be sure. Freedom and freedom-loving countries face a foe greater than the despotic and tyrannical ideologies of the 20th century. With the terrorist attacks on the World Trade Center and the Pentagon the conflict for the soul of the West has been engaged once again after 1300 years. It just may be that President Bush is the Charles Martel of the 21st century.

#4
TERRORISTS AGAINST MORALITY
October 4, 2001

On September 20, 2001, President George Bush spoke to the nation, and to the world, about the global terrorist threat and his resolve to bring it to its end. The terrorists are Islamic fundamentalists who believe that all the world's nations, whether they want to or not, should embrace Islam as the only way of life. The President addressed the need to reaffirm our values as the only way to deal with those whose values are so diametrically opposite to all America, to what freedom and democracy mean. His words took the form of a request: "I ask you to uphold the values of America and remember why so many have come here. We're in a fight for our principles, and our first responsibility is to live by them." Earlier he spoke of the terrorists as those who "abandoning every value except the will to power. . . follow in the path of fascism, Nazism and totalitarianism. And they will follow that path all the way to where it ends in history's unmarked grave of discarded lies."

These are stirring words, and impress us with the urgency of the hour and the core of the conflict—a struggle over abiding values. But the conflict over values did not begin on September 11, 2001, nor is it primarily associated with Islamic fundamentalism.

For several decades a terrorism against our values has been raging within America. It has insidiously woven itself into the very fabric of our way of life. It has goals similar to those of the terrorists who struck our country on September 11—to attack the heart of our culture and bring us down through moral decay.

I'm not thinking here of environmental or eco-terrorists, although the terrorists against our morals affects our environment. I'm not even thinking of racist terrorists, although racism and ethnic discrimination is evil. I'm thinking of "moral terrorists" who pervert our understanding of the good so that all the other terrorists can justify themselves in destroying property and human lives. There isn't a terrorist alive who doesn't violate the sanctity of property and the dignity of human life.

As Americans we want to protect the environment from noise and other pollution. We insist on clean air and water and soil. But what about the filthy speech, the cursing, and the swearing that pollute the environment, that are promoted by hollywood and the entertainment industry, that have surreptitiously crept into daily life in America, that flow from the mouths of children as soon as they begin to speak and never cease until their mouths lie silent in the grave? Out of the same mouths flow "God bless America" and "God d___ it." It is impossible that the God of love and truth can respond to one and not to the other. If we were to treat so-called friends with both blessing and cursing, we would no longer have any friends.

In the trivializing of our culture, we care more about disappearing fish and birds than about our children starving for lack of reality and the meaning of life.

We promote the values of freedom and liberty and justice for all. Yet we pervert freedom and liberty to license—license to kill and to destroy unborn life in the womb and the terminally ill, and deny the justice due to them. We redefine liberty by giving legal protection to pornography and other filth, and wonder why sexual crimes and exploitation abound. We give economic support to and legal protection of homosexual behavior. Our only concern is that the young are protected and that adults do it in a "loving" way. We salve our consciences about such love when God says there is no love in such behavior.

We speak of freedom to worship God as we please, and then find our pleasure in choosing not to worship or acknowledge him. We ban the saying of his name in prayer in our schools but defend the cursing of his name as freedom of expression.

We are terrorists all against the only kingdom which can give us the values to face the other terrorists of our day. We undermine it, we curse it, we ignore it. Even our churches, where God's kingdom is supposed to be our focused pursuit, tolerate behavior that God has warned against in his prophets.

So who are the real terrorists among us? First must come those who are able to enter every home in our country via the media, who are able to attack our innocent children and catch the rest of us unawares. The terrorists are the producers, writers, directors, actors, and talk show hosts who undermine our values by their filth and libertine lives—whose own lives are shipwrecks and empty of meaning and purpose. These terrorists use cunning and deceit to take multitudes captive. These terrorists take secret delight in their deeds. With smirks they poke fun at the values and decencies of our culture. They explore the most obscene and violent behavior for its shock value and ratings.

I say "real terrorists" to point out that the terrorists who struck on September 11 are those of the moment, who caused harm to the bodies of thousands but could not damage the souls of Americans. The real terrorists are those who through prolonged, insidious engagement have had decades to wreck their terror on us, and we are mostly unaware of the dangers. They are the real terrorists because they destroy the soul and heart of a culture; they soften it, compromise it, confuse it, weaken it, blind it. When once our values are gone we are easy prey for those of the likes of September 11.

These are the real terrorists because they undermine the values that have made us the greatest nation in history. They are the real terrorists because they, not Islamic fundamentalists, have the power to bring us to our knees. Isn't it ironic that the very freedom that flows from the values that have made us great and good—morality, respect for the dignity of the individual, reverence for God—the terrorists use this freedom to destroy the values which have fostered this freedom? Can there be any hope for such a self-destructive society?

These are the terrorists who invade our churches, schools and universities, government, and other institutions, and undermine what clerics, teachers and officials do. They promote a materialistic, secular worldview that denies the reality of the spiritual.

Now some will say that my comparison is not fair. Moral terrorists are not deliberately seeking to bring down our culture. Their intent is different.

In addition, they are not forcing their views upon the rest. Their ways are not violent or physical.

But I suggest that the moral terrorists do have the goal of changing our culture and institutions. They would redefine what is moral, good, and reverent. They deliberately rebel against the decided opinion of revelation, reason, and experience that asserts that you can no more invent a new moral standard than you can invent a new primary color. Their worship of the gods of success, excess, sex and violence are no less real than if they had made idols of wood, metal, or stone. And while they do not use physical force to implement their views, their influence via the media and institutions of prominence (the university) in our culture makes their power no less persuasive. Indeed, they know the power of ideas and suggestions; they know that to persuade the heart and mind is more enduring and effective; they know that they will be far more successful if people willingly embrace their corruption than if people are forced to adopt it. Their violence is not found in their tactics but in its moral equivalence—they embrace anarchy toward the good and the godly. They do not lay out their agenda for a democratic vote. They entice us with a facade of glitter and gold that hides the corruption behind the screen. They never tell us of the broken hearts, the broken homes, the broken lives strewn along the wicked path.

Do we still think that God will hear our prayers for help and guidance in our conflict with terrorists from abroad when we act like terrorists toward his kingdom among us?

So who are these terrorists? We are terrorists all, whenever we choose to live by values that undermine those that have made us great. Whenever we lie, cheat, use profane speech, extort wages and labor, lust and covet what is not ours, and commit secret sins of the heart we attack values that are essential to our life as a nation. While external terrorists will probably never bring down a free society, the internal terrorists have sown seeds for such destruction. We have become a nation of morally *sick* people. We are all terrorists because we have chosen to rebel against the constraints of God and his kingdom. What we give little or no place to Jesus said: "Seek first the kingdom of God" so that we will give proper place to everything else.

The real war in America today, as always, is being fomented by terrorists against God and his kingdom. If, as the President said, "Freedom and fear, justice and cruelty, have always been at war, and we know that God is not neutral between them," we can be sure that God is not neutral in the war between morality and immorality, between what is good and what is evil. The renewed interest in spiritual things is the first good sign that the war has not yet been lost.

#5
THE RELIGIOUS NATURE OF THE CONFLICT
WITH ISLAMIC FUNDAMENTALISM
Or
WHAT DO CHRISTIANITY AND ISLAM HAVE IN
COMMON?
October 19, 2001

President Bush has made it clear to the American people and to the world that our struggle against terrorism begun on September 11, 2001, must be waged on several fronts: economic and financial, cultural, with food, and with the military. Implicit also in his words was an acknowledgment that it is a spiritual or religious struggle. The terrorists have, he said, "hijacked Islam." They are "Islamic extremists" or "Islamic fundamentalists."

But what do such labels mean? How could a religion breed such people who would be willing to die as martyrs when they caused the greatest mass murder of civilians on a single day in our history, if not the world's? In order to understand the extremists we must understand Islam itself.

Islam follows the teaching of the Qur'an. Islam recognizes that Jews and Christians are also People of the Book. By this Muslims acknowledge that the Jews follow the teaching of the Old Testament and Christians follow the teachings of both Testaments. The Qur'an treats the People of the Book with considerable respect, and distinguishes them from pagans who do not worship the God of the Bible. Islam *claims* to worship the same God of the Bible whose name in Arabic is Allah.

All three religions claim to worship the God of the Bible. Yet this commonality does not mean that Islam affirms the legitimacy of a multiple or pluralistic approach to God. Nor do Judaism and Christianity. As a Christian I believe that the way of Jesus Christ is correct and that the other ways are in error. I believe that Jesus Christ is the only way to God: "I am the way the truth and the life; no one comes to the Father except by me" he said (John 14:6). I believe that the claims of Muhammad that he succeeded Jesus Christ as pointing the way to Allah are false.

But how each of these faiths deals with its claims of distinctiveness and exclusiveness is different. While each faith engages in witness, evangelizing, and proselytizing with the aim of making converts, Islam goes about this in a way that differs from Judaism and Christianity. Islam takes the position of reinterpreting the Bible contrary to the way both Judaism and Christianity have themselves interpreted it as the basis of their faiths, and supplants it with the Qur'an with its claims of superiority. In other words, Christianity sees itself as a successor to Judaism but does not reject the authority of the Old Testament. Indeed, Christianity embraces the OT as an authoritative pointer to Jesus Christ as the promised Messiah. In contrast, while Islam claims to believe the Bible and not to contradict it (Sura 2:136), it rejects the Christian interpretation of it. Islam puts the Qur'an in place of the Bible and claims that the Bible is corrupt whenever the Bible contradicts the Qur'an.

In other words, Muhammad invited others to examine in light of the Bible whether his teaching was true, so that the older revelation (the Bible) was the standard by which to judge the newer revelation (the Qur'an). But every time contradictions appeared, he rejected the Bible as untrustworthy. Such an approach is not only contradictory but a sham.

Tertullian, an early Christian church father (c. 160-225), argued that only Christians, not opponents to the faith, were in the position of defining what Christianity means. Only they could interpret Scripture correctly, because only they were in tune with its Author.

Applying this same approach to the conflict with Islam means that only Christians, not Muslims, are in the position of defining Christianity and interpreting who Jesus Christ is. In addition, Judaism and Christianity do not seek to extend the reaches of their faiths as measured in territory. In the present era the kingdom, Jesus said, is not of this world. He did not lay out plans for territorial expansion in the great commission (Matt. 28:18-20).

Christianity is supracultural. Yet Islam is wholly oriented toward establishing Islamic nations where the rule of *sharia* derived from the Qur'an and Islamic tradition holds sway.

Judaism and Christianity have no such designs on any nation. While the Crusades represent a time when Christianity had territorial designs, at least regarding the land of Israel, these *distortions* of Christianity and the Bible should not be compared to what is the *teaching* of Islam.

Wherever Islam becomes predominant it alters the culture of that country backwards to the culture of seventh-century Arabia. No place is allowed for the secular state, nor for the free exercise of other religions. The only democratic Islamic countries today are those where *sharia* is *not* practiced.

In addition, Muhammad often used physical violence, even murder, to force people to accept Islam. By example and precept Muhammad taught his followers to rob and kill. In contrast, Jesus prohibited his disciples from using physical force to advance his kingdom, and he never robbed and killed anyone. Instead he commanded his followers to love their enemies.

Now I said above that Islam seeks to reinterpret Judaism and Christianity. How does it do this? Regarding Judaism Islam claims that the descendants of Ishmael and not the descendants of Isaac are heirs of the promises made to Abraham concerning a posterity and a land. It asserts that the Jews have distorted the promise of Abraham to make it refer to Isaac. The Qur'an asserts that Abraham sacrificed Ishmael, not Isaac (Sura 37:100-112), and that he lived in Mecca and rebuilt the Kabah (Sura 2:125-127). Claiming that Islam is the only universalistic faith, it accuses Israel of being a "racist community." In the words of a Muslim, Ali Muhsin (in his *Let the Bible Speak*, 71), the Israelites of the Old Testament regarded themselves as the chosen people of God, "who had been granted the privilege to take other peoples (sic) lands and properties, by trickery when they were weak and by force when they were strong. . . . Legends were created under the guise of the Holy Scriptures which granted to the Hebrews the status of Herrenvolk." He goes on to assert that this same Old Testament provided inspiration to Hitler and the oppression of South Africa. He writes (p. 71):

Zionism is the spiritual ancestor of Apartheid and all other forms of Fascism. There is the legend of Noah cursing his son Ham, the ancestor of the Africans . . . and his descendants, to a status of slavery under the Jews and Europeans for eternity. (Genesis 9:18-27). By further scriptural manipulation the Jewish branch of the descendants of Shem had its status enhanced by having God establish his covenant with Isaac, as opposed to Ishmael who begot the Arabs. Could such a bigoted people to whom pride of race was everything, to whom the vilest of crimes were virtues sanctified by God so long as they resulted in the perpetuation and domination of their own race over others, could such a people—I humbly ask—be the carriers of a universal message? Most emphatically no!

Perhaps what is most disturbing about this quote is not its content (which is distorted in many respects and based on nothing factual regarding the "legends") but its spirit. If Islam is the final and only true faith, why does it betray its lack of confidence in its ultimate victory by such incendiary, inflamed language? Why must it resort to fabrications by accusing Judaism of creating legends and calling them Scripture, when there is no historical basis for such, and when Islam professes to follow the same Scriptures? Does not this spirit of triumphalism breed extremism? Clearly, Islam picks and chooses what it deems favorable to itself in the Jewish Bible, and then casts away or distorts the remainder—while at the same time it professes to embrace the Old Testament.

The attack on Christianity is similarly one of distortion and falsehoods. Probably almost everyone knows that Islam denies the reality of the trinity—God as three in one—and affirms monotheism or unitarianism. But contingent with this denial the Qur'an represents the trinity as consisting of God, Jesus and Mary. Islam also rejects the virgin birth of Jesus as God—the incarnation of deity; it denies that God has a special Son called Jesus; and makes Jesus created by God. It denies the reality of original sin or a sin nature; it denies that the atonement of Jesus Christ was a substitutionary sacrifice on behalf of others' sins; that is, it denies that Jesus took upon himself the sins of others. There is no salvation in him. Islam denies the resurrection as a sign of Jesus' triumph over sin, and it denies Jesus' final triumph at his second coming. It denies Jesus' eternal existence: he will finally die to be buried next to Muhammad in Mecca. Indeed, Islam denies that Jesus actually died on the cross, and asserts that some unknown person died there instead. Islam also rejects justification or salvation by faith. Rather salvation is by doing good deeds; everyone saves himself by doing what is morally right. Significantly, Islam claims that Jesus prophesied that Muhammad would come as the Paraclete, the comforter, of John 14:16-18, 26; 15:26; 16:7-15—passages that Christians view as teaching the coming of the Holy Spirit. It is Muhammad who convicts the world of sin, righteousness, and judgment (16:8). Finally, Muhammad, not Jesus, is the one Moses prophesied as the prophet to come like him (Deuteronomy 18:15, 18-19). Instead of putting faith in Christ we are to put faith in Muhammad and follow him.

All of these denials and assertions contradict what Christians believe about Jesus, and flatly contradict the clear meaning of the whole of Scripture. To bring about this reinterpretation of Christianity the Qur'an resorts to distortion of the New Testament or to claims of its corruption. It denies that John and Paul were true followers of Christ and claims that they were enemies to him and his gospel. The epistles of Paul, and of others, are rejected as spurious.

According to Allah, all who deny that these reinterpretations are divinely revealed by the Qur'an should fear the fire kept ready for the unbelievers (Qur'an 2:23-24). All false prophets should die (Qur'an 69:44-47). Clearly any who continue to maintain their commitment to Christ as Christianity affirms him is an enemy of Islam. This seems to contradict the great command of Jesus in the Sermon on the Mount to love your enemies (Matt. 5:44).

Islam means submission and a Muslim is one who submits to the will of Allah. While Christians also submit to God, they are also told by Jesus to address God as Father. Jesus also tells his followers that he would no longer call them servants (from the word *doulos*, "servant" or "slave") but friends (*philos*). The Qur'an never calls Allah "Father" nor are his followers called friends. Such intimacy is unknown in the theology of Islam. The Qur'an never identifies Allah with love as does the New Testament identify God as love.

The place of Jesus as God incarnate is the key to all reality and the biblical world view. Islam rejects such a place to Jesus. Hence they are not truly worshipers of Allah, of God. One can know God only by knowing Jesus as the physical embodiment of deity. The Scriptures say: "Everyone who goes forward and does not stay in the teaching about Christ does not have God. Everyone who stays in the teaching, this one has both the Father and the Son" (2 John 9). As Jesus said: "He who hates me also hates my Father" (John 15:23). God loves those who love his Son and believe that he has come from God (John 16:27). Indeed, to be in Christ is to be in the Father (John 14:10-11, 20; 17:21-23).

There is a movement afoot that would unite the three great faiths into one, that would synthesize them into one faith. The claim is that they all worship the same God. Not only is this misguided and untrue, but the intolerance exhibited by Islam in the past and taught in the Qur'an would insure that the only faith allowed must be the faith of Islam. Toleration for other religions would not be allowed. Until Islam bows the knee to Jesus as God's unique Son, Christianity can never be identified with Islam.

In an age and a culture that prizes freedom of religion and expression, that bathes in the luxury of pluralism, diversity, and tolerance, the one faith that cannot tolerate such values in a culture is Islam. It is not surprising that such a faith should breed the extremism of Islamic "fundamentalism" now catching fire among tens of millions of Muslims around the world.

What lies ahead on the horizon? It is not difficult to imagine a cataclysmic clash of civilizations, between the so-called Christian world and the Islamic world. The outcome will be either an unsettling impasse, or the success of the Christian world and a modified, redefined Islam exposed as a faulty faith, or the triumph of Islam with world-wide terror and the end of freedom.

#6
WHO OWNS THE LAND?
THE ARABS OR THE JEWS?
November 5, 2001

Certainly the weeks since 9-11-01 have focused attention on the conflict over the land of Israel as never before. While military action rages in Afghanistan and Central Asia, the war between the Palestinians and Israel has reached an intensity not seen since the unrest began in the fall of 2000. Why has the conflict erupted? What is behind the struggle over the land of Abraham? Who has the legitimate claim to the land?

The struggle over the land goes back thousands of years. About 1800 BC, according to the Book of Genesis, chapters 12-22, God promised to Abraham and his descendents possession of the land known then as Canaan. These passages reiterated the promise several times. The immediate descendents of Abraham were his son Ishmael, born to his concubine Hagar, and his son Isaac born to Sarah in a miraculous way (she had been barren until she was 90 years old). While Ishmael was promised a large posterity and territory around Canaan (Gen. 21:18), it is Isaac, according to the Hebrew Scriptures, who was to be counted as Abraham's seed and heir of God's covenant made with Abraham (Gen. 17:19, 21; 21:12; John 4:22). Isaac's descendents were to receive the land of Canaan and beyond (Gen. 21:12).

Yet the Palestinians, who are Muslim, protest this biblical history. Their hostility toward Israel goes back as early as the time of David, when Ishmael's descendents conspired with the Edomites (Esau's people) to oppose God and his people the Jews (Psalm 83), and said: "Let us destroy them as a nation, that the name of Israel be remembered no more" (vv. 3-8).

In the twentieth century, the Jews became the beneficiaries of a UN mandate that a homeland be created for the Jews on their historic place, along with a nation for the Palestinians. Hitler's Holocaust during WW2, during which about eight million Jews were exterminated, led the nations to decide for such a homeland. Israel fought several wars (in 1948, 1956, 1967, 1973) to secure their land. Although victorious, Israel willingly gave the Sinai to Egypt, and has progressively given more and more control of the Palestinian areas to the Palestinians. As late as 2000, Israel, under Ehud Barak, was willing to give back, in exchange for peace with her Islamic neighbors, much of the Golan Heights and perhaps other areas.

Yet the Palestinians and other Muslim extremists have refused to acknowledge Israel's right to exist, for the Jews to possess the land. They are not content to live in the West Bank and Gaza territory but they want all the land and they want Israel pushed into the Mediterranean Sea. Israel's attempt to build many towns in the West Bank over the last several years, to keep the Palestinians in check, only aggravated the Palestinians the more, and perhaps, with hindsight, was a wrong and a provocative strategy.

Now I admit that the preceding survey of history generally casts Israel in a better light than the Palestinians. I've tried to give an objective history, but many who favor the Palestinian cause will object. However, the basic question still remains: Who has the prior claim to the land?

The answer to the question, Jews, Christians, and Muslims agree, must take us back to the interpretation of the account of Abraham given above. The Hebrew Scriptures make Israel the recipients of the land. They are the descendants of Isaac, who was succeeded by his son Jacob who was father to twelve sons who became the patriarchs of the nation of Israel while living in servitude in Egypt. After the Exodus, the twelve tribes took the land of Canaan, conquering it by force and laying the foundation for the monarchy of David and his descendants. This partially fulfilled the promise of God to Abraham.

However, Islam rejects the Jewish-Christian interpretation of Genesis, and so rejects the Jews' claim to the land of Israel. Drawing from its Qur'an and traditions (the Hadith), Islam teaches that the true, correct descendent of Abraham is the other son, Ishmael (cf. Sura 2:125, 127). Abraham and Ishmael, according to the Qur'an, lived in Mecca (later to become the center of Islam in the seventh century, AD), and built up the worship centered around the Kabah and its black stone. Muhammad, the prophet of Allah, made the Kabah to be the new center of monotheism. Islam further claims that the Arabs, including the Palestinian Arabs, are the descendents of Ishmael, and that they should possess the land. Allah reveals his hostility toward Israel by calling them "cursed" and destined for hell (Sura 4:55-56).

Now whose "story" is true? Both cannot be true. It is the answer to the question, Who owns the land? that fuels the present conflict between Jews and Palestinians.

There are several reasons why the claim of Islam is false. The first is a biblical reason. When asked to give the basis of their interpretation of the Genesis account, Muslims reply that the present wording of the Genesis account has been corrupted by the Jews. They claim that the original text read differently and that the present Bible is unreliable in these places. Yet there is absolutely no basis for these claims. No one outside of Islam asserts such things. Muslims stand alone in these claims, and it is clear that they have ulterior motives. Islam distorts Scripture to give legitimacy to its claim of the land, to its hostility toward Israel, and to its claim that it succeeds Judaism and Christianity.

Islam faces a severe problem of logic at this point. On the one hand Islam appeals to the Genesis account as part of an inspired, authoritative text, and bases much of its religion in the Old and New Testaments (Sura 2:136). Then it turns around and denies the authority of portions of these texts that are in conflict with Islam. Islam cannot have it both ways: The Bible is authoritative, or it is not authoritative. How does Islam know that the portions that agree with its position are not corrupted?

There is also a historical reason to deny the Arabs' claims. There is no evidence in history or archaeology that Abraham was ever in Mecca. In addition, many believe that there is no evidence in the history of the Near East for the claim that the present Arabs are the descendents of the Ishmael of the Bible. So even if Ishmael were the designated heir of Canaan, the present-day Arabs have no claim. On the other hand, present-day Jews are in a direct lineage to Israel of the Old Testament. No one disputes this continuity.

The continuity in the Jews' possession of the land extends from the time of Joshua through David the King and his monarchy, then the divided monarchy, until the Jews were conquered by the Babylonians in 586 BC and the Temple destroyed. Under the edict of Cyrus the Persian, the Jews returned and rebuilt the Temple (in the fifth century); then they survived the conquest by Alexander the Great (fourth century) and the oppression of the Greeks under Antiochus Epiphanes (third century). They survived under Roman domination until AD 70 when the Romans destroyed Jerusalem and the Temple rebuilt by Herod during the time of Jesus. The Romans dispersed the Jews from the land after the rebellion in AD 132-135. Jerusalem was declared a Roman city and renamed Aelia Capitolina. A temple to Jupiter was erected on the holy site. From then until 1948 the Jews did not possess Israel.

This fact of continuity is a powerful argument. No one, and no nation, contested the right of the Jews to be considered the possessors of Canaan, or affirmed that the Arabs deserved it, for all sixteen centuries (from David until the 7th century AD), until the time of Muhammad. Neither the Egyptians, the Assyrians, the Babylonians, the Medes and the Persians, the Greeks, the Romans, nor even ancient Esau and Arabia, disputed the Jews' claim to the land. Does this not raise the suspicion that the claim of Islam is motivated by religious concerns and not factual ones?

But what is Islam's concern? Why should this be such a sore point for Islam? It is because Allah has decreed that Ishmael and his descendents are the heirs of the promise to Abraham, not the descendents of Isaac, the Jews. Since Allah cannot lie, and is absolutely sovereign and all-powerful, he cannot be wrong nor denied. For a Muslim it is not a reality that the Jews possess the land; it is impossible that the Jewish state should exist. Hence to ask Muslims to accept the right of Israel to exist is asking an impossible thing, a non-reality. It is blasphemy against Allah to call into question the interpretation of the Qur'an. For the Qur'an identifies Muslims as the "best of peoples" (Sura 3:110), while the People of the Book (Jews and Christians) need to put faith in Allah. Otherwise, they are destined for hell

So we reach this conclusion. Both Scripture, Scripture which Islam also endorses, and history decide the case for the Jews' claim to the land.

Yet there is something else to be said about the Muslim claim to be descendants of Ishmael. *Pursuit of the claim will mean the demise of Islam.*

Grave consequences await those nations occupying the land around Israel who oppress her.

So who are these nations? Genesis tells us that Ishmael and his descendents of twelve tribes went south from Canaan, to the east of Egypt (Gen. 25:12-18), the region which is now Saudi Arabia. In addition, the descendents of Esau (who separated from his twin brother Jacob, the patriarch of the Jews) settled to the southeast of Canaan, and came to be known as the land of Edom (Gen. 36:1-43). Indeed Esau bound himself to Ishmael by marrying one of the daughters of Ishmael (36:3). Many years later, the monarchy of Judah was overthrown by Babylon with the complicity of surrounding nations, including Damascus (the capital of Syria), Esau and Edom (both names are used), and Egypt. The prophets Isaiah and Jeremiah give extended treatment to a future day of judgment that will come on these surrounding countries for their complicity in the destruction of Judah and Jerusalem. Isaiah first singles out Edom (Isa. 11:14) for destruction, then, among others (chs. 13-34), Babylon, Assyria, Damascus (Isa. 17:1-14), Cush (southern Egypt), Egypt, Egypt and Cush together, Babylon again, Edom again (21:1-12), and then Arabia (21:13-17)! and again, for a third time, Edom (34:5-15). The promise is that God would use other more powerful nations, such as the Babylonians first, then the Medes (Isa. 13:17), to destroy them.

While this proclamation of judgment had a historical fulfillment, there is another fulfillment to come in the last days just before the LORD Almighty comes to reign in Israel (Isa. 24:21-24; cf. Ps. 102:13, 15-16). Peter claims that part of this section of Isaiah is fulfilled in Jesus Christ as the "precious cornerstone" (Isa. 28:16; 1 Pet. 2:6). Hence the prophecy reaches to Messianic times, to Jesus' time and beyond.

Similarly Jeremiah prophesies that God will use Babylon to destroy Egypt (Jer. 46:2-26), Gaza (47:1-7), Edom and Esau (49:7-22), and Damascus (49:23-27). Then Babylon will in turn be destroyed at the hand of the Medes (50:1-51:58). These prophecies were fulfilled. Yet Jeremiah's words also take on a greater dimension as he speaks of the last days and "forever" in these contexts (48:47; 49:6, 13, 33, 39; 50:5, 20, 39-40; 51:57, 62). God takes an oath, he swears, that such will be done (49:13; 51:14). Esau's destruction is compared to that of Sodom and Gomorrah (49:18).

Both prophets affirm a general pattern of history. By using other nations God punishes his people, the Jews, for their disobedience. But in vengeance (50:15, 24-28; 51:6, 11, 36, 49, 55-56) God uses yet other nations to punish Israel's oppressors. They become the tools of his vengeance. Indeed, God holds all nations accountable and will judge all that pursue evil. Though Israel is "full of guilt" God will not forsake her (51:5). This promise is not given to any other nation.

According to prophecy a great war will break out, known as the battle of Gog and Magog (see Ezek. 38-39; Rev. 20). Josephus, the first century Jewish historian, identified these names with the Scythians who inhabited the Caucasian region, now southwest of modern Russia, between the Black and the Caspian Seas. This area is strongly Muslim, as are the nations just to the East and the South: Iran, Iraq, Afganistan, Pakistan, etc. The terminology may also be symbolical of all nations determined to destroy Israel.

It just may be that the time of fulfilling ancient prophecies is nearer than we think. Following the earlier biblical pattern, the Muslim nations (the modern Egypt, Syria, Arabia, and Jordan) that occupy the land formerly held by Israel's enemies and that seek today to destroy Israel will themselves be destroyed by a greater nation (Could this be the US with her Western allies, or China?). Yet this nation itself will also be judged for its sins, just as Isaiah prophesied that all nations of the earth would be judged for their evil (Isa. 34:1-4).

Are we facing what may well be the final contest between Allah and the God of Israel? Surely one of the things that makes the God of the Bible angry, that blasphemes his name, is to see his holy place in Jerusalem profaned by the remarks quoted from the Qur'an and engraved around the Dome of the Rock. These words reject the idea of a trinity and the idea that God (Allah) should beget a son (Sura 4:171; 19:35). Yet Scripture says that God has highly exalted Jesus his Son and given him a name above all names (Phil. 2; cf. Heb. 1 where the Son is described in terms of deity). Whatever one's view of eschatology is, every Christian should be concerned over Islam's denigration of the Son of God.

Is this the time for purifying the US and the West? Only time will tell. All of us in the West need to take stock of ourselves and our countries, and repent of our rebellion against God. And Islam ought to be especially troubled by its opposition to Israel!

Some dismiss the question, "Who owns the land?" with another question, "Who cares? Let the Muslims have the land. It isn't worth fighting over, if it causes WW3." Yet in light of the patterns of history, we (the US) will have to choose to stand with Israel or with Islam.

To choose the latter will bring temporary relief, but only temporary. Not only will we incur God's judgment, but we will find that Islam will destroy our democratic, representative government and our basic rights and freedoms. Should we doubt this, the very fact that the Arabs are unwilling to reach a democratic, equitable resolution with Israel is a warning of things to come. Does anyone doubt that if a western nation were to become predominantly Islamic that freedom of religion would be jeopardized? There is not a Muslim country in the world that allows Christians to witness freely and to build enough churches to meet their needs. The freedoms of speech, press, and others will also go.

There are many Christians who deny that there is a special future place for the nation of Israel in God's plans. Yet even these people must respond to the question: "Is there no significance to the fact that over one billion people are united by one religion, Islam, to impose their religion and culture on the Christian West, and that Israel stands alone in the Near East as a barrier to the designs of Islam? Is this special place of Israel a mere coincidence, an accident of history? Believing as we do, that God is the Lord of history, argues instead that these events follow the old prophetic pattern. Whether we like it or not, on the horizon there is forming a cataclysmic clash between Islam and Christianity.

These are perilous times. Jesus himself rebuked the people of his day for not noting the "signs of the times"—to "analyze this present time" (Luke 12:54-56), and for not recognizing the time of their visitation (Luke 19:44). Jerusalem and Israel were about to be destroyed, Jesus meant, and it happened forty years later. Clearly we today should heed Jesus' charge.

God will accomplish his promises from old (Isa. 46:9-11). God will gather back to the land his people the Jews dispersed among the nations and will make with them a new, everlasting covenant (Ezek. 37:21-22) already begun in Jesus Christ. Jerusalem and Israel will be a stumbling block, a burdensome thing, for the nations in the last days (Zech. 12:2-3).

Who owns the land? God actually owns the land. And he has given it as a stewardship to Israel.

Why should any living person complain when punished for his/
her sins?
Let us examine our ways and test them, and let us return to the
LORD.
Let us lift up our hearts and our hands to God in heaven, and say:
"We have sinned and rebelled and you have not forgiven."

Lamentations 3:39-42.

#7
A CLASH OF CIVILIZATIONS:
AVOIDABLE OR NOT?
(rev. February, 2002)

A recent commentary by Grant Farr carried by the *Oregonian* (12-16-01) challenges the opinion held by some that the future will unleash a clash of civilizations that will pit the Christian West against the predominantly Muslim East. This is not a clash of politics or ideologies but of cultures, he affirms. Farr wants to be optimistic, that such a clash of civilizations is avoidable if we would only understand the issues differently. Yet his approach is typical of other secularists and revisionists who overlook much of history, minimize religious differences, blame the US for hostilities between East and West, and assert a moral parity between the two worlds. In addition, they ignore significant issues that are even more important than what they address.

Now such revisionists are helpful in showing the things that East and West have in common, and the failures of US foreign policy and influence, including the exportation of immoral values. Yet they make serious errors because of a deficient worldview.

First, such secularists assert that the West and East have more in common than what they do not, and that it is wrong to treat either side monolithically. Thus Farr writes that it is "just as unfair to say that Osama bin Laden represents Islam as it is to say Timothy McVeigh represented Christianity and the West."

But is it? Are these things on a moral parity? To my knowledge Timothy McVeigh never claimed to be a Christian or that he represented Christianity

36

or that he did his horrific act of violence in the name of Christ or that he found justification for his acts in the Bible. In contrast Osama Bin Laden has claimed all these things on behalf of Islam, Allah, and the Qur'an, and millions of Muslims agree with him.

Second, secularists revise history to suit their secular worldview and prejudice toward moral parity. To summarize almost 1500 years of history by saying that Jews, Christians, and Muslims lived peacefully together except for the times of conflict represented by the Crusades of the 11th, 12th, and 13th centuries is misleading and revisionist. To place the Crusades on a par with the history of Islam's conquests by the sword, tribute, or conversion, especially its attempts to conquer Western Europe in the 8th and 17th centuries, is distorted. Today there is no movement in Christian nations, calling them to conquer Islamic lands in the name of Christ, parallel to the call to Muslims to conquer in the name of Allah. Does anyone dare to suggest that Christianity or the West has made comparable attempts to conquer the lands of Islam?

Frankly I'm sick and tired of having pseudo-historians bring up the Crusades as examples of Christian aggression. They are not on a par with what Islam has done throughout its history and is pursuing once again in Israel, Indonesia, the Philippines, Central Asia, and Somalia. The parallels do not exist. The Crusades were attempts to *recover* the Holy Land from Islam, for Christians had exercised control over it from the time the Roman Empire became Christian in the 4th century till the time Islam took it in the 7th century. In addition, the Crusades represented an aberration, and, it could be argued, violated the command of Jesus himself to "love one's enemies." They are basically rejected today by all Christians as improper exercises of Christian power. No Christian statesman advocates their return. But Islam has never viewed its conquests this way, has never forsaken such a pattern or policy of conquest. Indeed, it is the Christian West that in the 20th century released the Holy Land as a home land for the Jews, and it is Palestinians and other Muslims who have sought to destroy Israel and deny her a right to exist. Egypt's former President Sadat was assassinated for thinking differently from the rest of the Muslim world.

Third, to assert that "it's really in the modern era, and especially in the past few decades, that tensions over cultural norms and values bloomed" (so Grant Farr) makes it convenient to blame US foreign policy again, with special attention given to our support of Israel. It is the old blame game—that Middle East violence is due to the US and we can hardly fault a violent response from terrorists. This kind of thinking allows the end to justify the means—including those used on September 11 that destroyed thousands of innocent civilians.

Indeed, the secularists deliberately brush aside the primacy of religious and attendant cultural values by asserting that *the root cause* of Muslim anger toward the West is American foreign policy. It is the "insensitivity and heavy-handedness of our foreign policies that have spawned their burning anger." They make the US a "big bully" and the Muslim anger toward us is "of our own creation."

The deficiencies of this secularist argument are clear. It is reductionist because it reduces several legitimate causes to one. Since Islam and Christianity are religions it is hardly a point of integrity to cite a secular reason for the conflict between them. The secularist argument is also anachronistic. Three hundred years ago there was no US to blame but there still was Muslim anger toward Christian Europe.

Fourth, and most importantly, it is an affront to both Islam and Christianity, and to truth itself, to gloss over the religious differences between Christianity and Islam. Secularists cast a blind eye toward deeply held beliefs. For example, one's view of who Jesus Christ is has significant consequences. Christians believe Jesus to be God incarnate while Muslims reject his deity. The difference is strategic, for it is Jesus who set forth the ethic of love. In the Sermon on the Mount he taught his followers to "love their enemies as they love themselves." Because he is God Christians are compelled to follow Jesus, to live in peace with their opponents. Because Muslims are not disciples of Christ they are not similarly compelled. Is it any wonder that Islam rejects or neglects his ethic of love toward enemies?

Finally, the great ideas of freedom, human dignity, and self-restraint under law that flow from Christian values are strangely absent from the secularists' vision of our past, present, and future. They make little attempt to raise the discussion to this level because they have rejected the basis for such values.

There have been other times when our values have been challenged. Shortly before the Civil War, John Quincy Adams argued before the US Supreme Court for the freedom of the slaves who had been brought over here on the ship *Amistad*. He reminded the justices that they must decide for freedom on the basis of our past heritage as expressed in our founding documents (the Declaration of Independence, the Constitution). Adams argued that the "inalienable rights" are derived from God and hence universally applicable. The Court, he asserted, must be swayed by these concepts even if their decision would bring the Civil War. In the end the justices decided for freedom, and for war.

The selling of this proper American dream is still the same. These values transcend cultures and we are (or should be) willing to die for them—to go to war if necessary. At the most basic level this is what the conflicts in Afghanistan and Iraq are all about.

Just a few days after the attack on America, on September 20, 2001, President Bush spoke to the nation and to the world about the importance of such values and the faith upon which they rest. He noted that the war on terrorism is about values such as freedom, justice, and democracy. God, he said, is not neutral in the conflict between freedom and fear, justice and cruelty. The terrorists who do evil in the name of Allah have blasphemed the name of Allah.

These great values sprang from the Christian West, not from the East or the Muslim world. Wherever *sharia*, or Islamic law, is instituted, there is no democracy or personal freedom on a par with what we enjoy in the US or West. *Sharia* accompanies totalitarianism. Along with many other freedoms, our most basic freedom, the freedom of religion, would be denied or severely limited.

These differences between the Christian West and the Muslim world are not just differing cultural values, and to be dismissed as such. These are fundamental values that transformed a barbaric West in the 4th century. The founding fathers of our nation embraced these values as universal, and it is this universality that has given them their great appeal. Their intrinsic goodness is recognized by all peoples whatever their cultural background.

Even in the way nations engage warfare there is a difference between the West and the Muslim world. On the basis of Christian teaching, the West has embraced the concept of "just war" that places limits on how warfare is pursued. This means that even in time of war we are driven by transcendent values. For example, civilians are not to be targeted during warfare; and there must be a probability of success when a nation goes to war. To my knowledge, and in light of the atrocities committed by the Taliban and others in Afghanistan and elsewhere, the Muslim world has not adopted these limitations. The terrorist slaughter of several thousand civilians on September 11 violates "just war." Indeed Islam is known for its *jihad*, or "holy war," that millions of Muslim people have embraced against the West.

These basic issues represent the contrasting worldviews of Christianity and Islam. It is time that the worldview of Islam itself be challenged. It is time for people to ask: What is it about Islam that encourages world conquest and totalitarianism? Is it not its view of Allah? Of the nature of people? Of the nature of government and political life?

The secularists use their American values of freedom to criticize America, while never lamenting the fact that such freedom is virtually absent in a predominantly Muslim state. They do not call for changes, for Muslim people to denounce contrary values.

Revisionists espouse their views because their own worldview is in conflict with the foundational values of our own culture which has been most influenced morally and spiritually by Christianity. These people have bought into a modern, secular, scientific worldview which promotes materialism, naturalism, and immoral behavior—the very values the secularists attempt to denounce!—and undermines spirituality and accountability.

The clash of civilizations is really a clash of worldviews. The worldviews of Christianity and Islam are at odds, and the worldview of secularism is bankrupt in trying to assess the nature of the collision.

Indeed, the secular view of history only validates the Muslim's complaint against the West—that we are a secular society that has lost its spiritual moorings and bred all sorts of evil. In other words, the secular view, rather than providing a solution to the problem, only exacerbates it. By its reductionistic argument that the "root cause" of Muslim anger is US foreign policy this view reveals the very decadence Muslims fault us for—failing to recognize the deepest claims of religious faith. A defective US foreign policy does not constitute a *root cause* but the *effect* of something else—a secular worldview. It is this that is a root cause, and secularists unwittingly promote it.

Most alarmingly, the secularists deprive us of the only thing able to win in the clash of civilizations—a superior moral position based in love, faith, and truth. By their misunderstanding and avoidance of the crucial role of religion to transform our culture, including our foreign policy, they invite realization of the very thing they hope will not come, the clash of civilizations, and our incapacity to meet it.

The clash of civilizations has a precedent in history. In the 5th century, decadent Christian Rome, while militarily superior to all others, fell to pagan invaders.

There is one basis for optimism, but it is not found where the secularists think. It is found in transcendent, spiritual values. It is they that have the power to transform our culture, and even Islam, along more just, generous, and beneficial lines.

If an apocalyptic clash of civilizations comes, it will do so not because of US foreign policy but because of a secular worldview that has rejected Christian values of dignity, truth, and spirituality. These derive from a divine presence in the universe.

#8
WHAT DO JERUSALEM, MECCA, AND ROME HAVE IN COMMON?
THE CHRISTIAN'S SEARCH FOR A CITY
Fall, 2002

The news about terrorist attacks continues to reinforce the fact that our world has risen to a new level of instability and insecurity. Since September 11, 2001, there have been terrorist attacks against, or terrorist cells exposed in, France, Indonsia, Yemen, Pakistan, Afghanistan, Iraq—just to name a few. The search for the perpetrators of crimes against civilians and children goes on. There is no foreseeable end to this crisis of civilization. The search for security and peace is goes on.

In ancient times the city was often built as a walled fortress. High walls, towers, secured entrances, and other reinforcements all made the city a safe place to seek refuge. In an agrarian world, at the time of war, people would leave their private homes and flee to the cities.

The world's greatest religions (Christianity, Islam, and of course Judaism) all hold in common a tie to the Old Testament and to Judaism. They all hold in common also a city of significance. For Judaism, it is Jerusalem.

For Islam, it is Mecca, the birthplace of Muhammad the prophet. While Medina and Jerusalem are also sacred cities, Mecca is the destination of all good pilgrims on the *hadj*.

For Christianity, there have been various sacred cities. Jerusalem, Antioch, Alexandria, Rome, and Constantinople have all vied for the honor. For the Roman Catholic Church the center of all authority, power and influence is Rome. From here the Pope makes infallible judgments. To here all the faithful around the world look for inspiration, direction, and security.

Each of these three great cities—Jerusalem, Mecca, and Rome—is a symbol of inspiration and reverence. They are also promises of renewal and hope for the future. If there is any security it will be found in such places. Just as in ancient times, the city provides security and deliverance. Or so it seems.

A little reflection leads one to realize that even these great cities are no more immune to attack and destruction than any other place. In modern times, the physical might of such centers is no more real than any other place. They are all vulnerable to weapons of mass destruction.

What about their strength as spiritual centers? To the faithful followers of each religion the centers do provide a degree of spiritual certitude. But they also stand as impediments to spiritual vitality and renewal. They comprise barriers as much as bridges. They are fortresses of strength and also fortresses of failure.

As I think about it, these three cities really reflect the natural way of looking at religion. They are magnificent in their position and prestige, in their tradition, but are antithetical to true faith. With the coming of Jesus Christ, and his kingdom, all has changed.

The Samaritan woman was overly concerned about the correct place, the city, to worship. She felt that Jerusalem was inferior to the Samaritan temple on Mount Gerizim. Jesus' stirring declaration set her back, no doubt, as it also does us. He said (John 4:2124):

> Woman, believe me, the hour is coming when neither on this mountain nor in Jerusalem will you worship the Father. You worship what you do not know; we worship what we know, for salvation is from the Jews. But the hour is coming and is now here, when the true worshipers will worship the Father in spirit and truth, for the Father is seeking such people to worship him. God is spirit, and those who worship him must worship in spirit and truth.

All other fortresses and securities are dissolved in light of Jesus' words. While many would suspect that the true worshipers of God are at a disadvantage, since they have no physical city to identify with, it is really an advantage. The physical cities bring with them limitations of language, culture, and ways of thinking. Jews have Hebrew, Judaism, and the traditions of the rabbis. Muslim people have Arabic, the culture of Arabia of the 7th century, and the absolute sovereignty of Allah, with no personal sovereignty. Roman Catholics have Italian, Western ways of rationalism, and the traditions and dogma of the church.

Evangelicals are different. They proclaim the good news of redemption and forgiveness of sins with no geographical marker. Following Jesus they carry the gospel from Jerusalem outward—to Judea, Samaria, and the ends of the earth. Evangelicalism can go anywhere and adapt the gospel to indigenous cultures, languages, and worldviews. Their message is a universal one, and their methods are universally adaptable. They do not need to look back to a city. Not even to Washington, D.C.!

And God intended this universalism from the very beginning. The nation of Israel sits geographically astride three great continents, bridging multiple cultures and peoples. It symbolizes the transcultural appeal of God's message of reconciliation for everyone.

Evangelicals should be wary of identifying any earthly city as home, whether it be London, New York, Washington, Tokyo, or any other place. No earthly city can match the promise of a better place.

Evangelicalism is the only truly global faith. Today there are over two billion Christians, and the fastest growing group are evangelicals. Judaism, Islam, and Roman Catholicism are all doomed to failure as long as they identify earthly cities as their centers. These centers symbolize natural religion.

We have here no city of security. As it has always been true, God himself is our refuge and strength. With the coming of Christ for the world, this great truth is actualized. He set the example.

Jesus himself turned his back on Jerusalem and Judaism when he willingly suffered rejection from the Jews (and from future Muslims and other Gentiles). He suffered outside the "gate" of Jerusalem in the place of uncleanness, rejection, and insecurity. But therein lay his strength and universal appeal. So we evangelicals must go where he has gone. The Scriptures say (Heb. 13:12-14):

Jesus also suffered outside the gate in order to sanctify the people through his own blood. Therefore let us go to him outside the camp and bear the reproach he endured. For here we have no lasting city, but we seek the city that is to come.

It is a weighty validation of evangelical faith that we have no geographical center. We alone worship God in spirit and truth. "Our citizenship is in heaven, and from it we await a Savior, the Lord Jesus Christ" (Phil. 3:20). In a very real sense we have already arrived in our essential identity as believers at the "city of the living God, the heavenly Jerusalem" (Heb. 12:22). It is this heavenly city, part of a heavenly country, and this alone, that God has prepared for his pilgrims from all the ages (Heb. 11:16)

#9
SO WHAT IS FREEDOM?
April 9, 2003

Today, April 9, 2003, the United States brought freedom to the Iraqi people. In downtown Bagdad, the statue of Saddam Hussein was finally toppled. As on April 9, 1865, when freedom was won by a great Civil War, so freedom came to another country far removed from us. But the freedom was won by the efforts and lives of a people who know freedom best among the nations of the earth. The people of the United States have passed the torch of freedom. Having ignited it, it will never be extinguished.

If Jesus Christ had not come there would not be a freedom won today in Iraq. If Jesus had not come, there would also be no United States of America, for it was founded and nourished by Christians seeking religious freedom. The Constitution of our country, the world's oldest democracy, promises rights that are endowed by the Creator. These rights are inalienable because they derive from God, not from government. The United States was able to bring freedom to Iraq because it owes its freedom to God, not to government. Freedom is God's gift, not America's, to the world.

The prophets of the Old Testament prophesy a future day of righteousness, justice and peace. It will be a day of freedom. It is ushered in by a military conquest such as the world has never seen. It is the coming of Jesus Christ. As our own country came into being through military conflict, so the new world order will be ushered in.

It is impossible to think of Christianity without Christ. It is possible to think that Islam could have arisen without Christ, if he had not come.

Yet the world would have been much different. Islam has not brought freedom anywhere, but instead total submission to Allah wherever possible.

There will never be personal or political freedom where Islam reigns. Just look at the world today. Only one or two of over forty Muslim nations are democratic. It isn't because of lack of natural resources; many Muslim nations have some of the greatest wealth imaginable. Rather the lack of personal and political freedom is due to their concept of God—how God is conceived in Islam. Until Islam receives Christ as divine and disavows total control of all of life, including personal living and the shape of the state, there will not be political freedom for Muslims. They are not personally, politically, and economically free because they are not spiritually free.

Why doesn't Islam grant freedom? Because freedom is threatening to its power, influence and core beliefs. Only Jesus Christ invited all people to search for truth wherever it may be found. And where people find truth, they find him, they find freedom. "You shall know the truth, and the truth shall make you free," he said. Islam cannot stand freedom because it cannot stand the truth. Islam is doomed to failure, sooner or later. Personal and political freedom go together.

Why is freedom so dear? What is freedom? Freedom derives from God. It is the consequence of a God of both justice and love, especially holy love. Freedom attends Christianity because freedom attends God. He risks releasing people to have freedom to choose rightly or wrongly. He knows that in the end people will choose rightly if they know the consequences of choosing badly and the bondage it brings. Freedom is a divine attribute. Certainly bondage is not. God is the most free of all beings in the universe, not free to do as he pleases, but because he always acts in agreement with his personhood—with what produces good, including freedom.

God has not revealed himself in Islam. Mohammad is not God's prophet. The very fact that the Qur'an never affirms explicitly that "Allah is love" proves the book is not from him. This is the difference between Christianity and Islam, pure and simple.

One cannot contemplate Christianity without Christ. But one can contemplate Islam without Christ, for in Islam he is considered a mere man, not divine, not a savior, not a resurrected Lord, not a returning

King. And the results of such are seen all over the world.

In retrospect, September 11, 2001, was an event that had to come. It alerted the world to the extremes of a religion and the horror it could propagate. It set in motion the direct conflict of Islam and Christianity on a par, perhaps, with the other two great periods of conflict between the two in the 8th and 17th centuries. Liberating Iraq provides the opportunity to demonstrate the differing values of two great religions. We will liberate Iraq, and then we will go home to allow Iraqis to discover the joys and institutions of freedom. We extend to others the very freedom we wish for ourselves.

Freedom does not mean license. For all to enjoy enough freedom, total freedom must be denied. The truth that leads to freedom rejects the lie that we can live as we please, without restraint. The truth exposes license as sin that leads to bondage, not freedom.

Jesus laid the foundation for political freedom when he approved the place for a secular government. "Render to Caesar the things that are Caesar's, and render to God the things that are God's," he said. Inherently, Islam has no place for the secular state. That is why it cannot promise political freedom and basic rights for all.

Without Christ there would not be a free country anywhere on earth. It is the values that flow from Christianity, not Islam, Hinduism, Buddhism, etc., that have made America what it is.

Prior to the Civil War, a French visitor to America made a profound observation about the greatness of America. Alexis De Tocqueville said: "America is great because she is good. If she ever ceases to be good, she will cease to be great." De Tocqueville was right on. It will be to our peril to forget this.

#10
TO AFGHANISTAN, *AND BACK*
A Report of My Experience in the U.A.E. and Afghanistan
Summer, 2003

In the late summer of 2003 I had the special opportunity to travel to Afghanistan. My trip had three goals: to visit and encourage some young women from our community who were teaching English in a university and an orphanage in Mazar-I-Sharif in northern Afghanistan; to investigate what skills are needed to help develop the country; and to discover what NGO's (non-governmental organizations) are there under which people could volunteer to work. All of these goals were met in some degree.

My traveling companion, John Graham, a retired civil engineer, was on his second trip to Afghanistan. He had been there a year and a half earlier, to draw up plans for a bridge over the Kabul river, and to do plumbing and electrical repairs in the city's major hospital.

My report is titled, "To Afghanistan *and Back*," because with all the negative and alarming news reports about travel to Afghanistan I had to reflect more than I had ever done before on the possibility that I may not make it back. In all my preparations, including contacts with my married children and their families, I carried this potentiality in my heart. Two of my children must have felt the same tugs at their hearts for they wrote me some very encouraging words.

My trip was brief, and I can only share impressions, for the most part, from my travels. Yet these are meaningful to me and I hope helpful to you the reader.

My experience in the United Arab Emirates and Afghanistan totally reversed my preconceptions about these two countries. I was completely surprised at the wealth of Dubai, a chief city of the U.A.E., and equally surprised at the poverty yet freedom found in Afghanistan. The initial shock of entering a new, different culture came at the airport in Gatwick, England, when I entered the door of the huge Boeing 777 plane of Emirates Airline. Immediately I was confronted by the appearance of most men as darker skinned and wearing turbans or other white "caps" that I had never seen before. Virtually every woman was wearing some sort of head covering—a scarf, or fuller headdress. As the plane took off and our long flight to Dubai began, I was struck by the wealth displayed in various ways, even in the décor of the plane. Indeed, the meals were elaborate (I chose a salmon dinner), the seats including the bottoms fully reclined, and the movie was free. The U.A.E. doesn't allow national women to serve as attendants, so young, attractive women are employed from all over the western world—from Australia, New Zealand, Great Britain, Ireland, and northern Europe. They go to great lengths to pamper every passenger. It is little wonder that Emirates Airline is rated the best in the world.

The trip to Dubai was merely a stop on the way to Afghanistan, but circumstances brought a team, including those from our community, of young American women and men from Afghanistan to Dubai. We spent five days there, debriefing and encouraging them in the use of their skills in Afghanistan. It was amazing to see how, after just three months, these young adults in their mid twenties had already adapted to a foreign, strange culture, were speaking some of the language, Dari, and were enjoying their opportunity and seeking to make the most of their six-month commitment to Afghanistan.

Twelve time zones away from Oregon, Dubai is an extremely wealthy place due to the production of oil. Several superlatives set it apart. It has the world's largest man-made sea port, which is visible from space; it has the world's tallest and only seven-star hotel (built on its own island in the Persian Gulf); it has the tallest skyscrapers between Europe and the Far East; it is the world's largest producer of aluminum; and it is constructing the world's tallest building. It also has one of the most oppressive summer climates: temperatures commonly reach over 45 C. (which is over 113 degrees F.) with about 80-90% humidity! The other seasons are much more comfortable.

The freeways are as modern as ours, or more so. The streets are filled with Toyotas as taxis, and many Mercedes and BMW's. The mosques are beautiful, and the five calls to prayer each day fill the air everywhere (as also in Afghanistan). Everyone knows English, so communication for Americans is easy. Thirty years ago there was virtually no modern city. Today under the leadership of its president and prime minister it is one of the most modern and wealthy cities in the world. In the Persian Gulf Dubai is developing a huge community on man-made islands that form the shape of the branches of a palm tree. Interestingly I discovered that the shopping centers, which rival any in the United States, have rooms devoted to prayer—one room for women and one for men. There is no democracy; there is no voting. The government was formed about seventy years ago when seven sheikdoms joined together to form the U.A.E.

Even though it is a major city in a Muslim country, Dubai appears to be quite liberal. Many nationals wear traditional dress (a white, full gown with turbans for the men, and a head-covering for the women; some women wear a complete black gown with head completely veiled). Yet many wear western dress, and many women go uncovered. Fully 75% of the working age population is comprised of immigrants—people from India, the Philippines, Pakistan, etc. The third world is coming to Dubai looking for jobs, which the nationals are willing to let them do. The currency rate is 3.5 dirhams to one dollar. The city is extremely clean, prosperous, and probably more free of crime than any large city in the West.

Just as much a shock is the poverty of Afghanistan, another half-time zone away. Ariana Afghan Airline is just gaining its stability. Flying on Ariana is the opposite of flying on U.A.E. Airline. Where Ariana doesn't fly, a Christian organization, Pac-Tech, fills the gaps. Pac-Tech flew our group from Kabul to Mazar. I was delighted to learn that all four pilots of the twin-engine ten-passenger planes were graduates of the same school from which I graduated in Chicago.

Clearly the Afghan culture differs from that of Dubai. Poverty is everywhere. The people dress differently and poorly, and speak Dari; hardly anyone knows English. The men wear a long tunic and pants of virtually any color, with a turban or white "cap." Probably half the women in Kabul wear only a head scarf; the rest wear a pretty-blue *burka* (covering the entire head and body, with only a small semi-opaque panel about 3 by 6 inches for the eyes). The material is completely formed of small pleats about a half inch wide (which I understand must be washed and ironed daily). In Mazar, northwest of Kabul, almost all the women wear *burkas*, but of various colors.

Kabul is a city greatly devasted by war, drought, and just plain neglect. It has endured twenty years of Soviet and war-lord conflict, followed by the oppressive atmosphere of the Taliban. What was once a beautiful city now has whole sections of the city in ruins. The Taliban forbade the education of girls and women, banned the theater and TV, required all women to be totally covered while in public and all men to wear turbans and grow long beards. There was antipathy for anything that seemed to compromise devotion to the Qur'an from a 7th century viewpoint.

Yet surprisingly there is now a welcome sense of openness to the West, especially America. One can almost breathe a new spirit of freedom in the air. There is little sense of insecurity, unruliness, or crime. I felt safer there, and I think a woman is safer there, than in most American cities.

The people have plenty of food, and it is inexpensive. Flat bread, rice with carrots and raisins, fruit, and tea make up the daily staples. The bazaars are filled with fresh food, including hanging meat, and clothing, utensils, and just about everything. The currency rate is about 50 Afghanis to the dollar.

Good water, while not available to most homes, is available everywhere in bottled form. All over the city of Kabul, along the streets, there are pumps on the tops of wells that some aid organization had drilled. This precious gift makes somewhat-pure water available to everyone. The temperature in late summer is about 100 degrees F., although the afternoons and evenings cool down in Kabul. It sits about 6000 feet elevation surrounded by mountains. Mazar is lower in elevation, hotter, and more arid.

The presence of military personnel from various Western nations isn't! That is, the military is in the countryside, not in the cities. They are there to keep the peace and to keep the terrorists at bay.

Guesthouses belonging to various development corporations are quite livable, having chairs, tables, computers, television, and running water. Native practice is to eat while reclining or sitting on *toshaks* (cushions) around the sides of a square oil cloth of sorts where the food is placed. I was reminded of the biblical practice of Jesus and his disciples who so reclined, as described in the accounts of the Last Supper. Electricity may go off or decrease each late afternoon, and comes on again around 9:00 pm. Relief organizations, and the pervasive UN, operate, for the most part, diesel powered Toyota vans and SUV's.

The entire infrastructure of the cities is in need of repair and restoration. And it is being done, mainly by aid from the US and the West. The story that isn't being told by Western media is how hundreds of private NGO's are providing free labor and materiel to rebuild the country. Hospitals, universities and schools, bridges, streets and more are being built or rebuilt with such aid. All kinds of people are there: doctors, nurses, dentists, engineers of various kinds, builders and construction workers, architects, carpenters, plumbers, well-drillers, teachers of English, computer programmers, teachers of children, day-care providers—the list goes on and on. It is a wonderful story of compassion by Americans and others. Because of the last twenty years of oppression and turmoil, most Afghanis are seriously behind their professional counterparts in the West.

Each of the cities has worship services and more for the Christian foreigners who have come to help rebuild the society. In Kabul, the main church has almost 300 attenders, although they meet in three or four smaller gatherings most of the time. Friday is the day of worship for Christians, following the Muslim custom. People in Afghanistan work five and a half days, getting Thursday afternoon and Friday off.

The most meaningful conversation I had while in Kabul occurred on our last night there. It was with a Muslim medical doctor. When he found out that I teach theology, he said: "I have a special interest in religion." For the next hour or so we conversed about many aspects of faith, including religion in America, and the differences between Islam, Catholicism and evangelical faith. Especially significant to me was his interest in the return of Jesus Christ. We have continued our conversation by email. I believe that this interest in evangelical faith is typical of many Muslims.

Our trip home involved five legs of flying, from Mazar to Kabul to Dubai to London to Cincinnati to Portland. It took us a total of almost four days to return, due to the difficulty of matching up arrivals and departures. The last part of our trip, from Dubai to Portland, alone took us twenty-eight hours both to fly and to wait for flights. This time and distance only reinforce the distance between the cultures of Afghanistan and America.

The opportunity for helping Afghanistan is now. The prayer for an open "door for the Word" is being answered now for Afghanistan. While Christians cannot go there as missionaries or even as tourists, they can go with an NGO and use skills to help rebuild the country. All kinds of skills are needed: medical, dental, engineering, construction, computer, educational, teaching, electrical, plumbing, electronic, agricultural, flying, business, marketing, and many more. By giving themselves in these ways Christians will demonstrate the love of Christ. Afghans will only be introduced to the Jesus of Scripture as personal relationships and trust are established. There is a great field ripe for the harvesting. Workers for this harvest are needed.

While I am happy to be back, I'm amazed at the tug of my heart to return—a feeling common to those who have gone. I'm convinced that now is the time to assist Afghanistan, and other Muslim lands. I'm also convinced that if many see what I have seen, and experience what I have, they would feel the same way.

PART TWO

THE RESURGING CHALLENGE OF THE CRESCENT
TO THE CROSS

THE ROLE OF THE HISTORICAL CRITICAL
METHOD, SECULARISM, AND GLOBALIZATION IN
ADVANCING ISLAM

INTRODUCTION

The horrendous attack of 9-11 on the United States by Muslim terrorists has kindled concerns, Western and universal, regarding the nature and designs of Islam. These include questions about the our nation's security, the relationship of Muslim terrorists to Islam in general, the ability of the West to pursue justice in many rogue states/nations, the growth of Islam at home and abroad, the relation of Christianity to Islam, and what the future holds. No one is able to foresee clearly all the possible ramifications.[3]

Some (for example, Samuel Huntington of Harvard, in his "The Clash of Civilizations," for *Foreign Affairs*; and Daniel Pipes) have written that the events fostered by Muslim extremists of the last few years portend a coming clash of civilizations along historic religious lines between the West and the Muslim non-West. This collision will affect world history and civilization in a destructive way.

These concerns suggest that the scope of the conflict may have eschatological import. Is the conflict a harbinger of the final end of the age? It would be foolish not to assess the "signs of the times," as Jesus warned us.

---

[3] There are several reasons why there is no assurance that the West will prevail in bringing the terrorist element of Islam to an end. There are millions of Muslims sympathetic to the cause of terrorism against the West; the terrorism is increasingly couched in religious terms as a war (*jihad*) against infidels, when before the attack the terrorism was basically secular (as in Iraq); the terrorism finds a fertile field among the hundreds of millions of people who live in poverty and who have nothing to lose but something to gain, especially Muslim honor; the higher birth rates among Muslim women compared to Western women; the history of past clashes between Islam and Christianity in the 8th and 17th centuries; and the increasing inability of the West to export spiritual values.

Of particular concern to Christians should be the resurgence of Islam and its challenge to Christianity. September 11 is a wake-up call to examine the religion that increasingly rivals Christianity for winning the hearts and minds of people around the world. Islam is aggressively pursuing its cause in comprehensive ways. Its apologetic is well-articulated, scholarly, attractive, and persuasive.[4]

Three developments in the modern era contribute to the resurgence of Islam in its challenge to Christianity. While the crescent has been in serious conflict with the cross for over 1300 years, it now pursues the case for its superiority with a vigor not known before.

The first development is the use within Christianity of modern historical-critical methodology in the forms of literary criticism and textual criticism. By adopting the so-called scientific method and its results as propounded by critics within Christianity Muslims are able to challenge the meaning and content of the biblical text and the doctrines of Christianity. This methodology plays a major role among educated Muslims in their elevating the Qur'an over the Bible in the esteem of Muslims and others.

From the beginning of its conflict with Christianity Islam has claimed that the Bible is composed of distorted or faulty texts and has imported legends and myths. The modern use of historical-critical methodology, with its foundation in rationalism and scientific theory, has given new impetus and legitimacy to this approach. This development constitutes the challenge arising within Christianity—the challenge to the mind.

The second development is the rise of secularism as the worldview of the West. The empiricism, rationalism, and scientism of modernism have fostered a worldview that embraces a secular view of reality, truth, and of what is moral behavior. Worldview determines all that we believe, including our doctrine and how we get it (hermeneutics, the interpretation of Scripture), and all our behavior. A secular worldview, arising in the West itself, poses the greatest threat to the success of Western Christianity in its conflict with Islam. The impact that this secular worldview has had on Christians is especially alarming. This development is the challenge arising outside of Christianity, from the West in general—the challenge to the heart.

---

[4] A resource containing scores of works dealing with Islam is the CD, "The World of Islam: Resources for Understanding" (Colorado Springs: Global Mapping International, 2000).

Introduction

The third development is modern globalization that contributes to the claim of Islam that it is the only truly universal faith. On the one hand, globalization is bringing technology around the world; and, on the other hand, it is increasing the disparity between the peoples who have (the West) and those who do not have (the non-West). Islam is perceived as the religion of the masses who are among the have-nots.

The most neglected factor in globalization is the role of religion, including Islam, among the peoples of the world.[5] The ability of the West to export the benefits of its culture, both material and spiritual, to answer the universal claims of Islam is the worldwide challenge to Christianity—the challenge to the will.

It is worldview that ties these three developments together. Worldview—how people view reality, truth, and ethics—determines how to deal with the historical-critical method, secularism, and globalization. A wrong worldview is the greatest handicap to Christianity, but a correct worldview is its greatest advantage.

These three developments of modern times pose significant obstacles to the ability of the cross to meet the challenge of the crescent, to convince of truth, and to claim the high moral ground. This study takes up in detail each of these developments and then evaluates them. In the conclusion I give some final suggestions on how to meet these challenges.

---

[5] Globalization involves political, economic, cultural, and religious factors. The most urgent threat to world peace is the spread of the means to build weapons of mass destruction, including biological, chemical, and nuclear weapons. Small groups, including radical Muslims, although relatively isolated and poor, could utilize such weapons.

THE EXPRESSION OF THE MUSLIM MINDSET

To show how these three developments are deeply embedded in the Muslim mindset I devote appendix one to a lengthy quotation from the preface of a Muslim work by Ali Muhsin. These three developments are repeatedly utilized later in his text.[6]

The preface sets forth both the approach and general tone of the writing. The author is convinced that Christians and Muslims worship the same God, and that pursuing the truth will lead to universal worship of him in the way of Islam. In subsequent pages Muhsin makes it clear that he believes that the meaning of the Old Testament, and its wording, have been corrupted, and only Islam contains the truth of the Old Testament. In addition, the Apostle Paul corrupted the teaching of Christ and the Apostles, who originally pointed people to the coming of Muhammad and his revealing of the universal faith expressed in Islam. Jesus never envisioned a gentile mission to reach the nations. He prepared the way for Muhammad to reach the world.

The author's view of the superiority of Islam is linked fundamentally to the view that the Gospels of Jesus are tradition that has been corrupted.

---

[6] Ali Muhsin, *Let the Bible Speak* (n.p.: n.d., n.p.). In these 81 pages the author seeks to show that Christians and Muslims have a common heritage and belief. Where they differ it is because the Apostle Paul has perverted the message of the Old Testament and of Jesus. The author identifies himself only as one who researched by "intensive Bible study" the meaning of Christianity from prison where he was held for ten and a half years, apparently in Tanzania. Apparently, Muhsin wrote this essay, but, according to the Forward, it was reviewed, retyped, annotated and corrected by the Dammam Islamic Da'wah and Guidance Center (p. 1). Its address is Dammam, Postal Code 31131—K.S.A. The quotations in the text above come from the preface, pp. 3-5, quoted in appendix one. While Muhsin's work may not be fully typical of all such apologetic works, it does seem to be a good representative of such.

This tradition is on a par with the traditions of Islam, which may also have been corrupted. Yet the Qur'an and what we have from Muhammad outshine the Gospels. "Jesus Christ has left for us nothing as authoritative as the Prophet Muhammad has done." The Qur'an has "unsullied purity" while the Gospels do not.

It is also clear that the author pins much of his viewpoint on the ability of reason and the modern scientific method to bring us to the truth. Three times in one paragraph of the preface the author refers to the role that scientific methodology can play. Indeed, the author claims that the traditions of Islam rest on better scientific study than do the Gospels when they were collected. In later pages the author makes it clear that this scientific study includes the conclusions of modern literary (higher) criticism and textual criticism. However, ultimate truth resides in the Qur'an and its "authenticity has never been questioned by friend or foe."

For Muslims worldview is paramount. Epistemologically, this worldview asserts that we should accept by faith that the Qur'an is ultimate, final, pure revelation; and that scientific methodology will help to secure and interpret the traditions of Islam beyond the Qur'an. Regarding reality, Islam affirms the realm of Allah as real, ultimate, and final. Finally, regarding the third area that a worldview addresses, the Qur'an and the traditions become the final source for what is moral or good . Submission to Allah is the basis for the moral behavior of people. Muslims are convinced that Islamic law, known as *sharia*, should govern wherever Muslims are in the majority and even where they are not.[7] Imposing *sharia* will bring the greatest glory to Allah.

The following pages take up the three developments identified above that, in the hand of Islamists, pose unprecedented challenges to Christianity.

---

[7] Norman Anderson, "The Law of Islam," *Eerdmans' Handbook to the World's Religions*, R. Pierce Beaver, et. al., eds. (Grand Rapids: Eerdmans, 1982), 322, points out that *sharia* has been classified under five categories: "what God has commanded; what God has recommended but not made strictly obligatory; what God has left legally indifferent; what God has deprecated but not actually prohibited; what God has expressly forbidden."

THE ROLE OF THE HISTORICAL-CRITICAL METHOD IN THE CHALLENGE OF ISLAM TO CHRISTIANITY

The beginning point of this assessment of the challenge of Islam to Christianity, of the crescent to the cross, must begin with its challenge to what we as Christians believe. By employing the historical-critical method, Islam rejects what Christians believe about God, Christ, the Holy Spirit, the Bible, sin, salvation, sanctification, heaven, hell, the future kingdom, and other significant doctrines. Muslims use arguments set forth by critics within Christianity.

Islam's Basic Beliefs

The basic beliefs of Islam are summarized by the "five pillars of Islam." (1) The confession (*shahada*): "There is no other God but Allah, and Muhammad is his prophet." The statement of this creed before two witnesses makes one a Muslim (note Sura 4:136). It is part of the call to prayer from minarets. (2) Prayers (*salat*) five times daily bowing toward Mecca. Before each time of prayer, ritual washing is prescribed. (3) Almsgiving (*zadat*). It is a tax amounting from 2 1/2 to 20 percent of annual income, depending on the source of wealth. It includes charity toward others to prevent poverty (yet some Muslim states languish in poverty along side very wealthy oil-rich states). (4) Fasting (*saum*) during Ramadan (the ninth month of the Muslim year), from sunrise to sunset. (5) Pilgrimage (the *hadj*) once in a lifetime to Mecca. The same practices once done by pagan pre-Islamic Arabs in Mecca are part of the ritual today.

Other summaries of the doctrines of Islam include the following.[8] (1) Belief in Allah as the one and only God. (2) Belief in angels (of four archangels, Gabriel is chief). Also every person has a protecting angel and two recording angels to record the good and the bad. There are also the *jinn*—male and female beings found in folk Islam. (3) Belief in many holy apostles and prophets (twenty-five are named in the Qur'an). Muhammad is the most important, the "seal of the prophets" (Sura 33:10). (4) Belief in the last day of judgment. At death the soul enters a state of unconsciousness until resurrection when Muslims will be judged for their deeds, suffering a brief time in hell. Eternal punishment is the lot of all who ascribed equals to God (e.g., Christians, Sura 4:48, etc.). (5) Belief in determinism: God predetermines both good and evil.

Islam's View of God.

Islam views God as Allah, and holds that he is the common God of Jews, Christians, and Muslims. The word "Allah" simply means "God." However, the term has its origin in the centuries before the birth of Muhammad. It is the name given to one of the 360 deities worshiped by polytheistic Arabic culture before the 7th century. Allah was a moon god identified by the symbol of the crescent shape of the moon. Muhammad was told by revelation that only "Allah" was the true God, and the rest were idols to be destroyed. Christian translators used the term "Allah" for the God of the Bible when later they translated Scripture into Arabic. This was more of a cultural rather than a linguistic decision.

Islam's Rejection of Christian Doctrine

For several pages, Muhsin clearly and correctly outlines Christian belief, the "teaching of the Church," as he calls it. This includes what the Church believes about God, the Trinity, the Father, the Son, the Holy Spirit, original sin inherited from Adam, baptism, the Bible, and redemption. Then he proceeds to show that all this has been distorted from the original truth found in Islam.

Islam rejects the idea of the Trinity as polytheism. Jesus Christ and the Holy Spirit are not divine persons. It is impossible that God should have a son. Islam distorts Christian belief regarding the Trinity by asserting

---

[8] William J. Saal, *Reaching Muslims for Christ* (Chicago: Moody, 1991), 34.

that Christians understand the Trinity as consisting of the Father, the Mother (Mary), and the Son, and that Christians worship all three as separate gods. There is no Trinity (Sura 4:171-172; 5:73-75).

How did the original truth regarding God (Allah) come to be distorted? The culprit is the apostle Paul. Paul's concepts of original sin and the need for redemption are wrong because they contradict the teaching of the Old Testament (which denies that a son should suffer for the sins of his father; Deut. 24:16; Jer. 31:29-30; Ezek. 18:19-20); and they contradict the teaching of Jesus (John 9:1-3).[9] Indeed, Paul's "revealed" version of Christianity was "fundamentally different from what the chosen disciples of Jesus knew to be the teaching of the Master, so that there was a serious conflict between Paul and original followers of Christ" who never deviated from strict monotheism.[10] Islam maintains that statements of Scripture suggesting a Trinity are later changes made to the text by Christians in response to Islam.

It is here that we get the first hints of Muhsin's appeal to higher criticism and to textual criticism that have been used within Christianity in modern times to pit Pauline theology against that of Peter and the rest.[11] Muhsin also utilizes the history of religions approach to assert that much of the Bible incorporates legends and myths from the surrounding religions.

Islam's View of Jesus Christ.

It is Islam's view of Jesus Christ that is most opposed to that of Christianity. The following outlines Islam's beliefs about Jesus Christ. (1) It denies that Jesus was preexistent and had a special virgin birth; rather he was created in the womb (Sura 19:22-26). (2) It denies that Jesus is God's special, divine Son (Sura 5:73-75; 43:81; 112:2, 3). (3) It denies

---

[9] Muhsin, *Let the Bible Speak*, 12. Why would the Church embrace Paul's teaching in contradiction to Moses, the Prophets, and Jesus? Muhsin can only say that the Church accepted Paul's epistles as part of the canon "for no earthly reason ." He later elaborates on this reason, as shown below.
[10] Ibid., 13.
[11] I summarize in appendix two the rise and influence of higher criticism, or the scientific method. By appropriating the results of the historical-critical method, Islam asserts that Paul's Epistles and those of others are spurious and corrupt, and that Paul corrupted the teaching of Jesus so as to make him divine.
The Qur'an does not mention Acts, nor the Epistles of Paul, Peter, James or John. Islam asserts that the New Testament as a whole is full of corruption and perverted texts, since we lack the original manuscripts.

that Jesus died as an atoning sacrifice innocently given for the sins of others. Rather Jesus died for himself, as a mere man. There is no salvation in Jesus. (4) The vast majority in Islam even deny that Jesus did die. Someone else died in his place (Sura 4:157). Instead the Qur'an refers to Jesus' future death (Sura 19:33; 3:54-55). (5) It denies that there is original sin or a sin nature with which people are born and for which they need redemption. (6) Though it allows for the resurrection of Jesus, it denies that such is a sign of his triumph over sin. He will be raised by God as others have been raised by God. Jesus is now in an inferior level of paradise. (7) It denies Jesus' final triumph at his second coming. (8) It denies that Jesus eternally lives, for he will die and be buried next to Muhammad. (9) It denies Jesus as God's final revelation and prophet (cf. Heb. 1:1-4); rather Muhammad is such. (10) It rejects justification by faith apart from works. Rather, salvation is by doing good deeds. Each saves oneself by doing what is morally right. (11) Salvation means to put faith in Muhammad and follow him, not Jesus, as the disciples supposedly did (Sura 5:110-111). (12) It denies to Jesus a special place at the end time. There will be a great war; Jesus will return as a sign of the times; he will reign for 24 or 40 years; he will convert Christians to Islam and eradicate all unbelievers; he will marry and have children; then Jesus will die and be buried in Mecca next to Muhammad (a commentary on Sura 43:61); then he will be resurrected to stand before God for judgment (Sura 3:55; 4:159). (13) It denies assurance of salvation. Every Muslim will spend a little time in hell. Then at the Judgment Muhammad will intercede for all Muslims so that, on the basis of their works, they will go to paradise. Only a martyr goes straight to paradise. (14) It does not equate Jesus with the coming of Mahdi (the "rightly guided one") who will institute universal Islam. (15) Islam connects the name of Jesus *('Isa)* with *al masih* (one who travels about as an apostle) from the Qur'an, but this does not have the same significance as the word "Messiah" (the Anointed One) in the Bible (Sura 4:171-172).

How does Islam come to its view of Christ that is so different from the Christian Church's view? Muhsin makes several arguments (parentheses include page numbers referencing his work).

Jesus Not the Son of God. First, it is clear that Jesus is not the son of God in some special sense. He is among several sons who are called such.

In addition, Jesus never called himself by this title, in the Synoptic Gospels, but preferred the title, "Son of Man," and viewed himself as a servant of God. Finally, Jesus was given names of divinity and invested with deity because in his time it was commonplace to invest with divinity not only mythological figures but historical mortals as well.

Muhsin cites the words of Francis Young in his works, *The Myth of God Incarnate*, and *Two Roots or a Tangled Mass?* as supporting his assertions (14-15). Muhsin goes on to show that others in the OT and in the NT were called "son" or "sons of God" (including believers in Christ), and that even individual people were on occasion called "god" (Exod. 4:16; Ps. 82:6-7). Finally, even John's usage (John 10:33-36; 20:17) shows that Jesus considered that his sonship was not different from that of others.

How did the Church come to view Jesus as equal with God? Paul and John have misled the Church by asserting a higher Christology. Yet even they distinguished Christ from God (1 Cor. 15:15; John 14:1; cf. Acts 7:56). In addition, Jesus prayed to and worshipped God (Luke 22:42-43), showing that they are "two separate beings of unequal status" (21). Also, the text shows that Jesus and God have two separate wills, with Jesus' will subordinate to God's; and while Jesus is weak, God is Almighty and the source of Jesus' strength. Finally, Jesus affirms that the Father is greater than he (John 14:28). Jesus' cry of despair from the cross shows not only that he is not God but that he displays a weakness that even an ordinary mortal with faith in God would not have.

The Miracles of Christ. How would Muhsin explain Jesus' miracles? His miracles are no different from others, for he does them by God's authority (John 5:30; 11:38-44; 12:49-50). Jesus acknowledges that miracle is for God's glory, not his; that God does it in answer to his prayers; and that God has sent him (22-23).

The Resurrection of Christ. Regarding resurrection, Muhsin points out that God raised Jesus. Jesus "did not rise of his own volition" (23). Nor was Jesus unique in experiencing resurrection (2 Kings 2:11). Furthermore, legends of people rising are "replete before and at the time of Jesus" (24).

The Virgin Birth. The virgin birth of Jesus is for people of faith. Jesus was created in the womb by Allah (Sura 3:59-60), but he was not the incarnation of deity (here Muhsin quotes Maurice Wiles in his article,

"Christianity without Incarnation?" (in Young's *The Myth of God Incarnate*) (24). For others outside the faith this doctrine is mythological; pagan deities prior to Christ claimed a virgin birth (e.g., the virgin Rhea Silvia gave birth to Romulus of Rome). Rationalists (such as G. Vermes in *Jesus the Jew*) fault using "virgin" as the translation in certain verses (Isa. 7:14) or of Mary. Finally, medical and scientific evidence shows that virgin births (accomplished without penetration of the male organ) can naturally occur (25-26).

Jesus As a Prophet. Jesus (Matt. 21:46; Mark 9:37; Luke 24:19; John 6:14; 17:3; Acts 3:13, 26; 4:30) and Muhammad (Sura 4:172) are equally prophets, servants, and messengers of God.

The Mission of Christ. Jesus was sent as a messenger to Israel alone not also to the Gentiles. He is not a redeemer of the world from sin (Matt. 10:5-6; 19:28; John 17:9). Out of personal ambition and force of personality Paul changed this mission to include Gentiles. Paul is the enemy of the gospel of Jesus (here Muhsin cites Marcello Craveri, *The Life of Jesus*; and Hugh Schonfield, *Those Incredible Jews*). Jesus sought to preserve the monotheism of Abraham from being contaminated with pagan influences all around Israel but Paul's work resulted in the law being cursed and Christianity absorbing all sorts of pagan cults (Mithra, Orpheus, Osiris, Attis, etc.). They became part of official Christianity. The Great Commission passages (not found in the original of Mark, the source of the other Synoptic Gospels) come not from Jesus but from Paul (1 Cor. 15:3-8). It is a legend Paul created. Likewise there is no basis for appeal to 1 John 5:7-8 to support the Trinity, since that passage is spurious (30-34).[12]

The Atonement of Christ. There is no salvation by the blood of Christ. Christ did not make a sacrifice for the atonement of the sins of others. The words, "He gave his life as a ransom for many" (Mark 10:42-45), are a figure of speech. John's declaration concerning the "Lamb of God" (1:29) is either an invention or a figure of speech meaning that Christ is the way of salvation by doing the will of God. He is pointing to the way to salvation, and hence Jesus (like others) becomes the savior of people. If Jesus as God died for the sins of mankind it is "stage-acting" for his death "meant nothing to him, for actually he did not die, being God" (36). It is a form of

---

[12] Ibid., 30-34. Here again Muhsin makes his claims based in higher (the historical-critical method) and lower (textual) criticism.

"outrageous cheating." If Jesus' death was predestined, then his killers should be hailed as "benefactors of mankind and the beloved of God" for fulfilling God's own desires (so also for Luke 1:68-71) (36).

It is "through righteousness, the doing of what is morally right, according to God's laws, that everyone will save himself" (37). As part of John's Gospel John 3:16 is not "intended to be a factual narrative, but rather subjective religious propaganda highly charged with sentimentalism" (38). Citing Schonfield (*Those Incredible Christians*) again, Muhsin asserts that John's book belongs among "several bogus books in the New Testament, and others which are purposefully misleading" (39).

The idea that another can bear our sins for us is "a doctrine of laziness" (66). These teachings come from pagan cults and pagan gods and their legends of redemption, atonement, and resurrection (66).[13] Muhsin cites Leo Tolstoi, *Appeal to the Clergy*, as supportive, that such ideas of redemption, etc., are contrary to reason (67).

Salvation By Faith Or By Works? Paul Or Jesus? Paul, who writes of justification by faith (Gal. 2:15-16; 5:4-5; Rom 3:28; 7:4-6; etc.), directly contradicts Christ who emphasizes "doing" in the Sermon on the Mount. Paul's proclivity to contradiction is seen in the three, contradictory accounts of his own conversion in the Book of Acts (42-44). Paul embraces the principle that the end justifies the means. Hence "by hook or by crook" he sought to win as many converts as possible and to undermine the claims to discipleship of Jesus' earlier companions (47). Paul is opposed to James (here Muhsin cites Hugh Schonfield, *The Passover Plot*) who "manifests the true spirit of Jesus" regarding the place of works. Paul is one of the false teachers and evil doers that Jesus warned about at the end of the Sermon on the Mount. When a contradiction between Christ and Paul occurs, we should go with the Master.

The Death of Christ. Muhsin goes to great lengths to avoid acknowledging the actual death of Christ.[14] Muhsin first appeals to an old manuscript recently discovered in Istanbul that identifies the early Christians as Nazarenes. These accused Paul of substituting Roman

[13] Here Muhsin cites in full the legends of Attis of Phrygia, Adonis of Syria, Dionysius or Bacchus of Greece, Mithra of Persia and Osiris and Horus of Egypt. Once again Muhsin is influenced by rationalism, the historical-critical method, and the comparison of religions school.
[14] Here Muhsin makes his most extensive appeals to reason and extra-biblical materials to bolster the statement of the Qur'an that Christ did not die. Higher and lower criticism are fully embraced.

customs for authentic teachings of Jesus. Judas tricked the Jews by betraying another man in Jesus' place, and it was this one who was tortured by the Jews and crucified. This explains the "pathetic lamentations" from the cross—they come from someone other than Jesus and are below the dignity of a leader (56). Muhsin goes on to quote Upton Sinclair (*A Personal Jesus*) that God becoming man is a legend (56-57). The man the disciples betrayed was "truly unknown to them"—hence they were not cowards after all (57)!

Muhsin gives other possible explanations for the apparent death of Christ. According to the Gospel of Barnabas, it was Judas who was crucified, not Jesus. The Basilidon sect of early Christianity claimed that Simon the Cyrene took the place of Jesus. Perhaps it occurred as H. Schonfield (*The Passover Plot*) describes it: Jesus was crucified, but he was drugged and did not die. Later he revived in the tomb. Even at the trial no proof could be given for the true identity of the accused.

Muhsin asserts that all this reasoning, the extra-gospels, and recent manuscripts corroborate the Qur'an (4:157): "for a surety they killed him not." Muhsin concludes: "In those same Gospels, there is also overwhelming evidence, in spite of the writers' own belief to the contrary, that it was possible, and indeed likely, that the crucified man was not Jesus Christ at all" (59). Muhsin boasts: "Modern Western scholars now accept the Quranic version of the story of Jesus" (60).

The Law and the License: Communion

After addressing the person and work of Christ, Muhsin turns to other matters. Jesus' mission was to fulfill the law of Moses, but the party headed by Paul taught that all that was necessary was merely "to believe that Jesus had died for them" (61). The communion, or Eucharist, or the Mass, is an outward ceremony to impress this role of faith on believers. Yet Paul originated it; it did not come from Christ. Paul's beliefs were made additions to the Gospels to have Jesus inaugurate the ritual! Proof that it comes from Paul is found in 1 Corinthians 11:23-26. The communion is "grotesque," "horrifying," and "a cannibal ritual" demanded by a "ruthless god" and having affinities with Orphic initiation (63; Muhsin here quotes Upton Sinclair and M. Craveri again, as above).

The Guide into All Truth: Muhammad

Jesus did not complete his mission but paved the way for another. He prophesied of Muhammad who fulfills all the elements of what Christians assign to the Holy Spirit (John 16:5-14). To read "Holy Spirit" in John 14:25 is an interpolation due to the "accumulated errors of fourteen centuries of manuscript copying" (49; he cites the editors of the RSV regarding textual criticism in general). Divisions in the Church show that none has the Holy Spirit. Muhammad is the promised "counselor" and is the "Spirit of Truth" (John 16:13). As a youth in Mecca Muhammad was known as the Al-Amin, i.e., the Truthful.

Muhammad brought the "proper perspective" (64). He reinstituted the pure Judaism of Moses, and cleansed Christianity of Paulinism. "Both were recast in their original imperishable mould of Islam" (64). Muhammad came with the Qur'an whose other name was "Furqan" or the "Criterion" which "distinguished truth from falsehood" (64). He granted "freedom from the Jewish restrictions but did not grant the license which Paul had unleashed" (64; see Sura 7:156-157).

Muhammad is of an exalted standard of character (Qur'an 68:4). He is described as the "Seal of all the Prophets and Apostles" (69). No other prophet arose historically after Muhammad to do God's will, to complete Jesus' task (70). Muhammad is final and universal. He came to abolish all tribal and racial faiths. There is to be "one faith for all men for all times" (70).

On the basis of his claim of textual corruption, Muhsin argues that Muhammad was prophesied as the "comforter" or "counselor" to come (John 14:26; 15:26; 16:7). He asserts that the Greek word in these texts (*paracletos*) has been misspelled from the actual, original word (*periclytos*), and cites "Christian" literary critics who affirm that parts of the Gospels are not historically true.[15] The new word means "the Admirable" (or, the "one who praises") and in Arabic is "Muhammad" or "Ahmed" or "Mahmoud."[16] Jesus is quoted in the Qur'an as saying that he was proclaiming "glad tidings of an apostle to come after me, whose name

---

[15] Muhsin cites the RSV as acknowledging mistakes in the manuscripts, and the scholars Rudolf Bultmann and Father John Lawrence McKenzie. Once again, Muhsin is appealing to the historical-critical method.

[16] Yet there is absolutely no support for such a change in the Greek text, and such a word exists in no Greek lexicon. In response to this Islam simply says that Muhammad is the comforter (see Sura 21:107; 9:128). The Holy Spirit mentioned by John is taken as the angel Gabriel (Sura 97:1-4).

shall be Ahmed" (Sura 61:6; 97:1-4). Jesus also prophesies the coming of Muhammad as the "rejected Ishmaelite stone," and the "rising of the Muslim Ummah (nation) to whom the Kingdom of God shall be granted" (74). God also prophesied to Moses the coming of Muhammad (Deut. 18:18-22): "I will raise up for them a prophet like you from among their brethren." The Arabs, descended from the Ishmaelites, are the brothers of the Israelites, and Muhammad is God's mouthpiece—the one of whom God said: "I will put my words into his mouth" (Deut. 18:18).

The "quality more pronounced than another" in Muhammad was the "wonderful fulfillment of all what he foretold" (78). Muhsin cites a few examples of "the devastating exactitude of the fulfillment of his prophecies" (79).[17] Apart from Muhammad there has been no one else in history on a par with Moses (79). The Qur'an (69:44-47) and the Bible (Deut. 18) alike promise death for the false prophet.

The servanthood of both Jesus and Muhammad "met in Islam . . . the religion that has no beginning and no end, for it is the religion of nature" (80). Muhsin quotes Geoffrey Parrinder, *Jesus in the Qur'an*, as acknowledging the "undoubted revelation of God in Muhammad and in the Qur'an. . . . The example of Islam towards other people of the Book often puts us to shame" (81).

The Qur'an

How important is the critical method to Islam's claims regarding the Qur'an? It both has, and does not have, a significant place. In the first place, Muhsin faults the Bible as containing "forgeries, manipulations and deliberate inventions" (52; Muhsin again quotes Hugh Schonfield, *Those Incredible Christians*). Christians use evasions to explain such forgeries or they assert that the author is someone in the Pauline or Petrine school of thought, or they are "secondary" sayings (52). In contrast, Muhsin

---

[17] Interestingly E.B. Pusey, *Daniel the Prophet: Nine Lectures* (n.p.: Funk & Wagnalls, 1885; rep. Minneapolis: Klock & Klock Christian Publishers, 1978), 509-511, contradicts certain claims often made that others have prophesied just as reliably as Daniel. One of these claims is that Muhammad himself predicted the Muslim conquest of Constantinople that occurred in 1453. Pusey shows that there was no such actual prophecy about Constantinople; that Turks, not Arabs, took the city; that it fell in an ordinary way, not a supernatural way; that it was besieged contrary to the supposed prediction; and that it fell not as supposedly predicted. "Every detail of the prediction is directly contrary to the fact" (511), he observes.

quotes Sir William Muir as writing two hundred years ago that the Qur'an is like "no other book which has remained twelve centuries with so pure a text."

Regarding the canon of the Bible, Muhsin (citing Schonfield again) says that truthfulness was not a concern in establishing the books. The canon is disputed.

Regarding inspiration, Muhsin asserts that there are no originals of the Bible. The present books are the works of many, ordinary human writers. While some words are of divine origin, they are mixed with many that are not so that it is impossible to tell the divine from the human (53). In contrast, every word of the Qur'an is Allah's—his direct speech, not just inspired. The official text was established in accordance with the dialect of Mecca under the third caliph, Uthman.

The Qur'an challenges anyone to prove that any chapter was composed by man. After 1400 years no man or spirit has yet taken up the challenge (76). The Qur'an, Muhsin asserts,

> is the standing miracle of Muhammad . . . a miracle for eternity, a book inscribed, a Guidance to mankind. You can read it today, tomorrow and forever. You will be inspired by the grandeur of its style, by the wisdom and learning which it embodies, and by the loftiness of its moral and spiritual teachings.

Muhsin cannot contain his praise for the Qur'an. It is the book for the past as well as for the modern era of science and knowledge.[18]

---

[18] Muhsin claims that monotheism comes from Muhammad. His conception of God as presented in the Qur'an "impressed the notion of the strictest monotheism upon the pages of history and towards this notion rational man cannot but drift surely if slowly" (77). This book made the Muslims "the founders of Algebra, Chemistry, Astronomy and Modern medicine at a time when Christian Europe was busily engaged in the futile controversies" of religious debate. This book enriched the learning of Greece, Persia, India, China, and Egypt. It "urged individual effort"; it made "the seeking of knowledge a compulsory religious duty to every male and female"; it "changed the sun, the moon and the stars from being objects of worship to objects of study, subservient to man." It is the "Book that liberated the intellect of man, and widened his scope of enquiry into realms hitherto undreamt of" (77).

The Teaching and Distortions of Islam Regarding Judaism

Regarding the patriarch Abraham Islam embraces several positions that are at odds with the views of Jews and Christians.[19] (1) It asserts that Islam through Ishmael, not Judaism through Isaac, is the heir of the promises of a land and seed made to Abraham. (2) It asserts that Abraham attempted to sacrifice Ishmael, not Isaac. (3) It asserts that Abraham lived in Mecca and rebuilt the Kabah.[20] (4) It asserts that Judaism is racist, and that Zionism breeds Fascism. (5) It asserts that the Jews have distorted the OT Scriptures to their view. (6) It asserts that the Arabs are descendants of Ishmael.

Muhsin minces no words in his view of Israel. He not only exalts the role of Muhammad to unite all peoples under a universal faith, but he tears down Israel as an unworthy people to represent God as the God of all the peoples. Israel is a "racist community" (70), and Zionism is "the spiritual ancestor of Apartheid and all other forms of Fascism" (71). How did Israel come to view itself as the chosen people? They created legends "under the guise of Holy Scripture" and by "further scriptural manipulation" (71). Muhsin denies that such a "bigoted people to whom pride of race was everything, to whom the vilest of crimes were virtues sanctified by God so long as they resulted in the perpetuation and domination of their own race over others" could ever be the "carriers of a universal message" (71). Rather, it is the Arabs, an international people, who are capable of intermingling with others of diverse racial origins, because they combine both Hamitic and Semitic sources (since Ishmael was himself born from an African woman from Egypt).[21]

Is Allah the God of the Bible? This is a crucial question addressed in the evaluation section below.

---

[19] See Elishua Davidson, *Islam, Israel, and the Last Days* (Eugene: Harvest House, 1991), 24ff.; Robert Morey, *The Islamic Invasion: Confronting the World's Fastest Growing Religion* (Eugene: Harvest House, 1992), and Muhsin.

[20] There is no biblical or archaeological evidence for Abraham in Mecca. See Morey, *Islamic Invasion*, 23-24.

[21] The hostility of Muhammad toward the Jewish people probably derives from the fact that, even though they are viewed as "people of the book" (as Christians also are), they refused to respond to Muhammad as a prophet of God. To account for differences between the Jewish faith and the Qur'an, Muhammad charged the Jews with corrupting their scriptures, for perverting the words. The same charge was made against Christians. See Christy Wilson, "The Qur'an," *Eerdmans' Handbook*, 315.

THE ROLE OF A SECULAR WORLDVIEW IN THE CHALLENGE OF ISLAM TO CHRISTIANITY

The second cause for a resurging Islam is the growth of a secular worldview in the West. Worldview is the most crucial aspect of Islam's new challenge to Christianity.[22] How one views reality, and God as ultimate reality, is fundamentally different between Christians and Muslims.

Yet these differences should not cloud the great similarity between Islam and Christianity on the issue of worldview. Both are committed to the unseen realm of God as the ultimate realm of reality. However, Christianity in the West is in danger of having embraced a secular worldview from the culture so that its capacity to present a powerful challenge to Islam is impeded.

The worldview of Islam is perhaps best summarized by appealing to the meaning of "Islam." Originally "Islam" was an Arabic word referring to manliness, and described someone heroic and brave in battle.[23] The word slowly developed into meaning "submission." A Muslim is one who is submitted (note how "s," "l," and "m" are basic to Islam and Muslim (see Sura 4:125). Thus the Islamic worldview places Allah at its center. All reality, truth, and the good derive from Allah and he determines all. Hence the basic confession of Muslims, "There is no god but Allah, and Muhammad is his prophet," articulates the foundation of their worldview.

Characteristics of Islamic thinking and worldview include the following. (1) There is no secular realm or division between church and

---

[22] In his article, Charles Colson, "Drawing the Battle Lines," *Christianity Today* (January 7, 2002), 80, rightly sees the conflict with Islam as being first and foremost a clash of worldviews.
[23] Morey, *Islamic Invasion*, 36.

state. (2) Islam embraces time as a wheel having a cycle of a hundred years.[24] (3) The goal of Islam is to make one *umma* of the people of the world, an Islamic people in submission to Allah. (4) All the world is divided into two parts: Dar-al-Salaam (House of Peace), "in submission"; and Dar-al-Harb (House of War), what is not "in submission." While in the minority in certain countries, Islam has a "third domain," an "area of agreement" or political compromise—gently confronting people with the claims of Islam.[25] Those who have not yet been brought into "submission" are subject to *jihad*. (5) Islam is to become the state religion, and the *sharia*, the law or constitution of Islam, is to control all aspects of life.[26]

Saal cites the following as defining the Muslim worldview: submission; Allah's absolute transcendence; human goodness; divine guidance from the Qur'an and Hadith and other sources; a community of "The Submission" (*Al-Islam*)—a new world order, the Community of Islam (the *Ummah*); and a heavenly culture of divine origin which is derived from the belief that the Qur'an came down from heaven in the heavenly language of Arabic (hence the Qur'an can't be translated; all prayers and ritual are in Arabic; and converts take Arabic names; etc.).[27]

Saal's mention of "a new world order" and "a heavenly culture of divine

---

[24] Davidson, *Israel*, 84ff. As Islam declines toward the 50-year mark, it experiences a 50-year resurgence, but backwards towards its beginnings, not forwards. The years 1950-2000 are a time of resurgence, with the Ayatollah Khomeini beginning his revolution in mid century, and eventually taking over Iran.

[25] Ibid., 13.

[26] September 11 was a demonstration of how far Muslim extremists will go in seeking to purify Islam. While such are angry at the West for a perceived oppression their primary goal is not to punish the West but to purify Islam. They are not angry at the degraded values that the West is exporting but are angry at their own Islamic states' failure to adopt *sharia* and practice pure Islam.

I'm indebted to Mr. Galen Currah, a missionary for many years among Muslim peoples, for the preceding observations. Yet, one must keep in mind that, in many respects, Islam is more cultural than religious. In the words of Morey (*Islamic Invasion*, 20-32), Islam is the deification of 7th-century Arabian culture which is to be imposed on all other cultures. This would mean that there would be (1) no democracy, no civil rights; (2) prayers toward Mecca and the pilgrimage and dietary laws; (3) the woman's veil and denial of basic rights to women (Sura 4:34); and (4) cruel and unusual punishment: incarceration without due process; torture, political assassination, cutting off of limbs, ears, tongues, heads; and gouging out of eyes.

[27] Saal, *Reaching Muslims*, 42ff. This culture became the center of world civilization in the tenth century, has declined since the 1700's, but now is experiencing resurgence since World War 2 because of independence from colonial powers, the discovery of oil, and rapid demographic growth (doubling every 24-30 years).

origin" especially reinforces the aspect of worldview that seeks to define reality. Yet the worldview of Islam is not unsullied. Throughout the world today there are many Muslims who do not submit to Allah in the form of 7th century Arabic culture. Nor do all Muslims abide by all the religious elements of their faith and seek a "heavenly culture."[28]

Values are a significant expression of worldview. Patrick Cate reminds us that values drive people to live and think a certain way.[29] While Westerners, with their secular worldview, value individualism and liberty, separate between their public and private lives, and focus on materialism and the physical, Muslims value just the opposite. In many ways Muslim values may be closer to biblical values than Western ones are, and closer to those of Christians.

Cate separates Muslim values into the categories of the theological, animistic, and the cultural. In the first category Cate places the unity of God, the sovereign free will of God, submission and man's response to God, the Qur'an,[30] and Muhammad.[31] Animism is the belief that supernatural powers reside in animals, nature, and objects. Underneath this belief, Cate notes, are "the driving values" of fear and power. Muslims believe in a personal Satan and demons, called *jinn*. From the latter come

---

[28] Dr. Nabeel Jabbour, a Christian born in Lebanon and educated in Egypt, in remarks made to the Evangelical Missiological Society at its northwest regional meeting at World View Center, March 9, 2002, Portland, Or., gives seven types of Muslims: (1) folk or popular (influenced mostly by the culture and tradition) ; (2) secular (educated, modern); (3) orthodox (know and hold to the doctrines of the Qur'an); (4) contented (glad to be born a Muslim rather than a Jew or Christian); (5) ignorant (often influenced by superstition); (6) mystic (emphasize the vertical relationship and the horizontal); and (7) fundamentalist (most committed).

Jabbour identified three influences that make one a fundamentalist: understanding *jihad*, understanding what it means to follow Muhammad, and understanding what it means to be unworldly.

J. Dudley Woodberry, "The War on Terrorism: Reflections of a Guest in the Lands Involved" (unpublished paper distributed at the same meeting of the Evangelical Missiological Society referenced above) says that a "fundamentalist" is one who goes back to the fundamentals of his faith—the Qur'an and practice (*Sunna*) of Muhammad and the earliest Muslims—and reject later adaptations. "They hold that their understanding of the society of the earliest Muslims is the model for society even today, and it applies to all areas of life" (2). Militants may be peaceful or militant, he adds. The Muslim Brotherhood are pious and idealistic, and will commit terrorism to meet their goals.

[29] Patrick O. Cate, "Islamic Values and the Gospel," *Bibliotheca Sacra* 155 (July-Sept 1998): 355-70.

[30] Cate, ibid., 356-60, points out that the Qur'an is authoritative for a Muslim because it is "the uncreated speech of God existing in the mind of God from eternity past" (358). The other sources of authority are the *Hadith* (traditions), *Qiyas* (analogy taught by Muslim scholars and based on the authority of the first two), *Ijma* (the consensus of the community and especially of Islamic scholars), *Adat* (the custom of the community, from which comes animism), and *Qanun* (international law).

[31] Cate points out that Muhammad is the one who "has central—or single—authority" in the lives

the powers of the evil eye.[32] Some Muslims use the Qur'an in divination and believe that intermediaries can cast spells of blessing or cursing. They wear amulets to ward off the power of the evil eye and the *jinn*.

The cultural values of Islam include the *Umma* (the Muslim community), family and marriage, hospitality, and honor and shame.[33] Honor is such a high value that it transcends telling the truth. One may lie and deceive in order to avoid shame. Hence it is not surprising that the Qur'an teaches that Allah himself practices deceit.[34] Good relations are more important than the truth. Muslims do not struggle with guilt for having sinned before God but with shame and bringing dishonor to one's family or to oneself. "The preservation of self-respect is of the highest value."[35]

The values of honor and shame affect how the good is pursued and the role of truth. Any means can be pursued to attain or avoid these values. If the end is to preserve at all costs honor, personal or family, then the means to preserve these values could include lying, theft, and even murder.

The concept of universalism in the worldview of Islam deserves special attention. Muhsin comments that Muhammad abolished "tribal and racial discrimination, and instituted a new brotherhood, the brotherhood of faith, and the brotherhood of man" (71). Two early followers of Muhammad were Zaid and Salman, converts from Christianity (71). The reason Islam spread like "flare fire" was because Muhammad taught a "universal God, a universal religion, a universal brotherhood" (72). Muhsin appeals to the role of belief, but belief of a special kind (72). This belief makes Islam a universal faith superior to Judaism and Christianity. He writes (72):

It was not mere belief that did the trick; it was the type of belief,

---

of Muslims (360). He points out that in "almost every mosque two words are written in Arabic at equal height above the ground"—the names of "Muhammad" and "Allah," with the latter always on the right. To speak against the prophet or the Qur'an is blasphemy and justifies the use of capital punishment in many Muslim lands.

[32] Ibid., 362.

[33] Ibid., 364-68.

[34] Ibid., 357-358. Cate asserts that three times the Qur'an teaches that God deceives and that God is the best deceiver (Sura 3:54; 8:30; 10:21). The attempts to translate the words involved as "plot," "plan," or "the best planner" do not do justice to the full meaning and as defined in Hans Wehr's standard Arabic dictionary. There the term *makara* is defined as "deceive, delude, cheat, dupe, gull, or double-cross" and the term *makir* is defined as "sly, cunning, or wily."

[35] Ibid., 368.

belief in works, belief in the brotherhood of man and the universality of God's religion. From the Atlantic to the Pacific, from the Caucusus to the Comores, from Senegal to Sinkiang, from Istanbul to Indonesia, all became one brotherhood, all had one all-embracing ideology, all faced towards Mecca, all mixed their bloods and cultures so that differences in race, colour and tongue became completely meaningless. The youngest of all the great religions became the only truly universal one. The only racial groups resisting the attraction of Islam have been those which at all cost would insist on maintaining their racial purity and alleged superiority, and thus have been the greatest contributors to the racial animosities which bedevil the world of today. They are fighting a rearguard action.

Belief in the "universality of God's religion" gives Islamists their universal perspective. This universalism ultimately derives from a worldview and the conviction that the spiritual is the most significant aspect of reality. A secular worldview denies that faith in God should be universal.

It is precisely here that Christians should be particularly alarmed by their own compromise on this point. A secularist worldview has come to dominate much of Western living and deeply affects Christian, evangelical living. This compromise impairs Christians' response to the Islamic challenge regarding worldview.

A recent newspaper opinion piece illustrates how our culture has embraced a secular, pluralistic worldview. The author attempts to deal with the challenge of Islam from such a viewpoint.[36]

Grant Farr ("Colliding Cultures," *The Oregonian*, 12-16-01) wrote his piece to challenge the opinion held by some that the future will unleash a clash of civilizations that will pit the Christian West against the predominantly Muslim East. It is not a clash of politics or ideologies but of cultures, he affirmed. Farr wants to be optimistic, that such a clash of civilizations is avoidable if we would only understand the issues differently.

Farr's approach is typical of other secularists and revisionists who overlook much of history, minimize religious differences, blame the United

---

[36] See my fuller critique to the secular response to Islam in "A Clash of Civilizations: Avoidable Or Not?" Unpublished article, December 20, 2001.

States for hostilities between East and West, and assert a moral parity between the two worlds. In addition, because of a deficient worldview they ignore significant issues—values derived from the spiritual realm—that are even more important than what they do address.

The approach of the secularists includes several points. First, they assert that the West and East have more in common than what they do not, and that it is wrong to treat either side monolithically. Thus Farr writes that it is "just as unfair to say that Osama bin Laden represents Islam as it is to say Timothy McVeigh represented Christianity and the West."

One must always beware of monolithic misrepresentation.[37] But are these things on a moral parity or equivalency? To my knowledge Timothy McVeigh never claimed to be a Christian or that he represented Christianity or that he did his horrific act of violence in the name of Christ or that he found justification for his acts in the Bible. He never claimed that he sought to purify Christianity. In contrast ObL has claimed all these things on behalf of Islam, Allah, and the Qur'an, and millions of Muslims agree with him.

Second, secularists revise history to suit their secular worldview and prejudice toward moral equivalence. Farr summarizes almost 1500 years of history by saying that Jews, Christians, and Muslims lived peacefully together except for the times of conflict represented by the Crusades of the 11th, 12th, and 13th centuries. This is misleading and revisionist. To place the Crusades on a par with the history of Islam's conquests by the sword, tribute, or conversion, especially its attempts to conquer Western Europe in the 8th and 17th centuries, is distorted.[38]

Third, secularists assert that "it's really in the modern era, and especially

---

[37] Again Nabeel Jabbour, in his remarks made at World View Center (see note above), reminds us that Islam is both peaceful and militant (not one or the other). It is like a rope having five strands: Muslims are a people; a culture; a worldview (the lens through which they view reality) including such values as honor, courage, hospitality, generosity, loyalty, etc.; a theology or system of belief; and an evil structure of power based in fanaticism.

[38] Today there is no movement in Christian nations, calling them to conquer Islamic lands in the name of Christ, parallel to the call to Muslims to conquer nations in the name of Allah. The Crusades are basically rejected today by all Christians as improper exercises of Christian power, as aberrations, and, it could be argued, violations of the command of Jesus himself to "love one's enemies." No Christian statesman advocates their return. Indeed, it is the Christian West that in the 20th century released the Holy Land as a homeland for the Jews, and it is Palestinians and other Muslims who have sought to destroy Israel and deny her a right to exist. Would anyone dare to suggest that Christianity or the West is making comparable attempts to conquer the lands of Islam?

in the past few decades, that tensions over cultural norms and values bloomed" (so Grant Farr). Indeed, the secularists deliberately brush aside the primacy of religious and attendant cultural values by asserting that *the root cause* of Muslim anger toward the West is American foreign policy. It is the "insensitivity and heavy-handedness of our foreign policies that have spawned their burning anger." The United States is a "big bully" and the Muslim anger toward us is "of our own creation."

The deficiencies of this secular position are clear. It is reductionist because it reduces several legitimate causes to one. Since Islam and Christianity are religions it is hardly a point of integrity to cite a secular reason for the conflict between them. The secularist argument is also anachronistic. Three hundred years ago, the time of the last great clash between Christianity and Islam, there was no American policy to blame but there still was Muslim anger toward Christian Europe.

The old blame game is still alive, asserting that Middle East violence is due to our support of Israel and one can hardly fault a violent response from terrorists. This kind of thinking allows the end to justify the means—including those used on September 11 that destroyed thousands of innocent civilians.[39]

It is in regards to a secular worldview that Christianity is most vulnerable to the challenge of modern Islam. It is the perception of many Muslims that Christians in America are only superficially religious.

---

[39] Below, I present further deficiencies in the secular worldview

THE ROLE OF GLOBALIZATION IN THE CHALLENGE OF ISLAM TO CHRISTIANITY

The third cause for a resurging Islam is globalization. In several ways the matter of globalization overlaps the thoughts expressed in the preceding section regarding a secular worldview and the universal designs of Christianity and Islam.

It is appropriate that faiths which claim universality should consider the causes and effects of globalization. For one thing, no one and certainly no religion can escape globalization. The world is becoming interconnected as never before. The events of September 11 witness to such connectedness. The terrorists came from far away, and the American response has landed troops halfway around the world.

As seen above, Islam takes special pride in being a universal faith. It seeks global domination because Allah would be most pleased as this is realized.

How is it that Islam has spread to the degree that it has? Strangely, the oppression that many Muslim people endure today is the direct result of Western influence. During colonial days the British, French, and Dutch often prohibited Christian missionaries from entering their Muslim colonies, such as northern Nigeria and Indonesia, in order to keep the people servile. Allowing Christianity among such peoples would encourage unrest, liberation, and nationalism. Thus Islam came relatively recently to Indonesia as it took up against the Dutch the banner of nationalism and independence.[40]

---

[40] Again, I am indebted to Galen Currah for these observations. On the other hand, the exportation of freedom can be one of the greatest accompaniments to the exportation of Christianity and its values. In those countries that are predominately Muslim today, Christianity is growing because it often represents freedom from oppressive regimes. The events occurring in Afghanistan witness, in part, to this phenomenon.

While many from a variety of disciplines are writing about globalization, few admit a place to the role of religion, and even fewer compare Christianity and Islam in respect to globalization. Yet some are beginning to do so, and I find that some of my concerns are voiced by them as well. I cite two who write as evangelicals, and one who writes as a Roman Catholic.

Globalization is difficult to define, but defining it is crucial. Gordon Lewis discusses various definitions, including a global village, a world economic order, international capitalism, and Americanization. He defines it more broadly to include worldwide dispersion of economic, social, political, cultural and religious ideas.[41]

Lewis' major contribution, I think, is his exposure of the role of religion in globalization. He identifies Christianity and Islam as the two "most effective globalizing religions," both of which are rooted in Judaism.[42] Lewis cites Roland Robertson, perhaps the "most important and creative globalization theorist," who affirms that both merchants and Christian missionaries sparked the current rise of globalization during 1875-1925.[43]

---

[41] Donald M. Lewis, "Globalization, Religion and Evangelicalism," *Crux* 38:2 (June 2002) 36. He cites seven common elements in scholarly thinking (36-37). (1) Globalization is a "cultural and economic phenomenon" rooted in "the expansion of European nations" and the "universalizing religious impulse of Christianity." (2) Globalization is linked to the rise of modern capitalism in the 18th and 19th centuries. (3) International capitalism has triumphed as an economic system. (4) Globalization involves the diminishing of barriers, traditions, universal claims, and identities (although Lewis questions these assumptions). (5) The future of the nation-state is a key issue of the debate (some believe it will dissolve). (6) A global culture is unlikely but geographical location will not determine how people will act (Lewis cites the possibly changing face of Islam here). (7) Cultural, political, economic and social analysis must operate not at the level of the nation-state but at the global level.

Lewis goes on to distinguish between globalization as a description of what is happening, the various theories about why it is happening, and the impact it may have. He issues several cautions (38-39). (1) We need to distinguish between what is happening and what appears to be happening. (2) We need to identify the assumptions people import into the discussion. (3) We need to distinguish between description and prediction. (4) The range of views of globalization include the cultural, the economic, and the social-political. (5) Globalization can produce powerful counter movements and reactions. (6) Globalization may be adapted to local conditions (what Roland Robertson calls "glocalization"). (7) Globalization is often being accompanied by postmodernism, leading to a questioning of traditions (religious, cultural, and political).

Lewis affirms three implications of globalization that most theorists can agree upon (39-40). These are (1) international migration; (2) continued growth of key or global cities; and (3) reactions against perceived threats arising from identity crises.

[42] Ibid., 40.

[43] Ibid.

Weber, the "father of modern sociology," identifies Calvinism with its "rationalization" as that which ignited capitalism as an expansive, international force.[44] The universe was demystified, and modernization and secularization soon followed. While many believe that religion is thus marginalized and loses its importance and impact, both Robertson and Weber believe that just the opposite may happen. Religion may experience resurgence and become a spoiler of globalization.[45]

Certainly the recent rise of Islamic fundamentalism is viewed as such a spoiler by its adherents. The polemic by Ali Muhsin discussed above provides the theological underpinnings for this fundamentalism.

Lewis' special contribution is to point to evangelical Christianity as the only globalized religion. He cites statistics to show that Christianity in general now has about two billion adherents, or about 33-34% of the world's almost six billion people.[46] He attributes Christianity's growth in the last half of the twentieth century to the expansion of Pentecostal or charismatic evangelicalism in the non-Western world. Evangelicalism has been able to "harness lay initiative" leading to indigenous, culturally diverse, popular Christianity—an unplanned religious "glocalization."[47] Islam cannot expand this way, being impaired by several localizing demands: one language (the Qur'an cannot be translated but must be learned in Arabic); one holy place (as one of the five pillars of Islam, everyone must make a pilgrimage (the *hadj*) to Mecca; and one name for Allah (indigenous translations are not accepted).[48]

I would add that Islam, by seeking to impose *sharia* worldwide, rejects indigenous cultures and seeks to impose a seventh-century Arabian culture on the rest. While Christianity has sometimes been wrongly syncretized with pagan traditions, only Christianity shows an amazing adaptability to local traditions. This universalizing tendency began with the Old Testament prophets (cf. Isa. 49:6ff.), was commanded by Christ (Matt. 28:18-20), and was brought into effect by Pentecost and the council at Jerusalem (Acts 2 and 15) that distinguished between essential beliefs and non-essential traditions.

---

[44] Ibid., 41.
[45] Ibid., 41-42.
[46] Ibid., 43.
[47] Ibid., 44.
[48] Ibid.

Lewis concludes by addressing the future of evangelicalism in a globalizing world. He sees the three trends of international migration, global cities, and reactions against globalization as continuing to aid the spread of evangelicalism.[49] While religious liberty has not been as strong a trend, globalization may bring more openness and freedom of choice, with evangelicalism being one of several new religious options for many people.

In a way similar to Lewis, Max Stackhouse points to a neglect of religion in discussions about globalization. At a spring, 2001, conference on "The Ethical Challenges of Globalization," Stackhouse spoke to the question: "Is God in Globalization?"[50] He sought to evaluate the book, *Global Transformations*, considered the "definitive work on globalization" by social scientists. The latter identified three major, competing views of globalization: the economic, proposed by "hyper-globalists" who see economics uniting the world and bringing an end to hunger and nationalism; the cultural, proposed by anti-globalists who believe that a "retribalization" is promoting national and cultural pride faster than globalizing influences; and the political, transformational view that holds that a changing shape of power is sweeping the world.

Strangely, as Stackhouse points out, the social scientists devote only two pages in *Global Transformations* to the role of religion. They virtually ignore the place of religion, faith, theology, or ethics. Hence they are left with an incomplete explanation of the causes, the spread, the reception, and the resistance to globalization. Their definition of the nature and character of power itself excludes the unseen, spiritual forces at work and believed to be most important to people of faith (whether Christians, Muslims, or others). Stackhouse observes that the "moral and spiritual architecture of every civilization is grounded more than any other factor in religious commitments that point to a source of ultimate meaning beyond the political, economic, and cultural structures themselves."[51] Stackhouse believes that Christians should use their resources to fill in

---

[49] Ibid., 45-46.

[50] His remarks, in shorter form, were reported in the newsletter of the Center for Applied Christian Ethics of Wheaton College called *Discernment* (summer/fall, 8:2/3, 2001) 2-4. Stackhouse is an editor of the multi-volume series, *God and Globalization*.

[51] Stackhouse, "Is God in Globalization?", 3.

what the social scientists ignore so that "globalization can be a blessing and not a curse to humanity."[52]

Stackhouse raises important questions. In our present global era, when all religions must encounter each other, whose religion will prevail? Which religion and which foundations do we want to shape the future? While Christianity has sometimes been allied with evil forces, and Christians need to repent of this, they should not shrink from seeing globalization from a Christian theological perspective. Islam certainly has its global designs. We should embrace the claim in the New Testament, Stackhouse writes, that Christ has brought the unseen forces and authorities "under the laws of God so that they can, in the long run, serve the purposes of God as a part of the mercies of God, and that all believers in Christ are called to be agents of this reconciliation process, especially in a global era for the glory of God."[53]

C.A. Casey, a Roman Catholic sociologist, pleads for globalists to recognize that religion (or, transcendent reality, or truth) is the foundation for freedom, not an obstacle to it.[54] He begins with interpretations as to the cause of the events of 9-11, and faults those who fail to recognize the role of globalization and religion. He critiques those, such as John Gray, who define globalization as Western modernity. They assert that Western modernity has become the new, secular religion which is replacing the modern state and marginalizing traditional religion. Gray believes that 9-11 is a rejection of Western modernity and globalization.

Casey seeks to clarify the relationship of globalization and religion. He cites various warnings from the Pope that, while globalization in itself is neither good nor bad, transcendent reality is necessary to turn

---

[52] Ibid. Following various passages of Scripture (apparently, for example, Col. 1:16; etc.) that address these matters, Stackhouse and his colleagues identify the spiritual "powers," the "disembodied potentialities," that become resident in social, political, economic, cultural, and personal life. They also identify the "principalities," "authorities," and "dominions" in all societies. Some of these powers are universal, some less so. Others are primary and necessary for society, for the right ordering of civilization, and others are potential threats to the right shape of society.

[53] Ibid., 4. How do Christians do this? Stackhouse suggests that, first, Christians need to recover how faith influences the structure and institutions of life. Second, Christians need to "develop a fundamental theory of how to order complex systems." Third, Christians need to develop people who have a deep memory of "biblical and theological history" and who "have a profound commitment to being God's agents in the midst of a rebellious world."

[54] M.A. Casey, "How to Think about Globalization," *First Things* 126 (October 2002) 47-56.

globalization to serve the human person, solidarity, and the common good. It must serve, not subvert, freedom and the truth. Without the foundation of truth, freedom exposes people to violence and manipulation, and the market economy becomes an "unending contest of power."[55] Casey counters those who view religion, particularly Christianity, as irrelevant or an obstacle to globalization and democracy. Casey cites the Pope who affirms that religion provides the values to keep democracy from becoming totalitarian. Democracy demands a community that embraces moral norms, moral truth. Without these the human spirit does not triumph but dies. Freedom's need for moral truth is not Western-specific but basic to human life and culture everywhere.[56]

Casey then critiques the relationship of Islam to democracy, and comes to conclusions similar to mine (see below). Statistics from Freedom House reveal that of the forty-seven Muslim countries less than one-fourth are electoral democracies. Only one, Mali, is rated as a free country. Muslim states make up seven of the ten least-free countries. Muslim countries make up the majority of non-free states in the world.[57] Explanations for this situation cannot appeal to poverty or even Islamic extremism. Rather, the lack of freedom arises from the hybrid nature of radical ideology reflecting a "perverse form of engagement with both modernity and the West."[58] Casey traces the origin of this radicalism to the Muslim Brotherhood founded in Egypt by Hasan al-Banna in 1928. The radicalism was advanced by the Egyptian Sayyid Qutb (1906-66), "the intellectual mentor of modern Islamism."[59] Islam rejects Western-style consumerism as an attack on its culture and religion, and a humiliation. Islam views the rule of unbelievers (*dar al-harb*—the house of unbelief or war) over believers (*dar al-islam*— the house of Islam) as "blasphemous and unnatural."[60]

Casey observes that the lack of freedom in many Muslim countries is not just lack of national independence but lack of freedom for the individual to choose his actions. This is directly attributable to the nature and definition of Islam as "submission." The individual is free only to choose to submit to

---

[55] Ibid., 49.
[56] Ibid., 51-52.
[57] Ibid., 52-53. The statistics are for 1999-2000.
[58] Ibid., 53.
[59] Ibid.
[60] Ibid., 54.

Allah, to his sovereignty. The West's concept of the sovereignty of the people is irreconcilable with the sovereignty of God.[61] Christianity puts stress above all on loving God and others (the two great commandments, as Jesus described them), which leads to concepts of responsibility, freedom, and the human person quite different from those in Islam. With no church, the individual is exposed to greater domination by society. With no separate warrant for a state, the state is not rooted in society. With the family as the only corporate unity recognized by *sharia*, the state is vulnerable to capture and corruption by powerful family networks.[62]

Thus, Casey observes, Islam's impact on certain states represents a critical obstacle to globalization, and an important challenge. Islam needs to develop a concept of the person that, along with the attributes of love and reason, accepts freedom as a part of human nature. Islam tends to view freedom as something external, along with law and morality, to be imposed by the will of God, rather than as formulations written on the heart.[63] In other words, I would add, Islam fails to embrace the new covenant as realized in the coming of Christ. At the same time, Islam needs to develop clear boundaries between the public and religious domains, as the New Testament does.

Any secular attempt to resolve these issues is doomed to failure. Casey concludes that the West needs to overcome its secularism and recover the vital role of religion in securing freedom. For globalization to bring freedom and prosperity to non-Western cultures, globalization needs to take religion seriously. Freedom cannot succeed without religion. Religion is the cornerstone of freedom.[64]

Christians dare not consider globalization apart from the religious element involved. Indeed, the faith of a people is the most important influence in culture.[65] Both the Lord's Prayer, asking God to extend his

---

[61] Ibid., 54, 56.

[62] Ibid., 55.

[63] Ibid., 56.

[64] Ibid.

[65] Even the agnostics, Will and Ariel Durant, argued in their massive study, *The Story of Civilization*, that all civilizations are characterized by four features: a system of economics, a system of politics, education and the arts, and public morality. In their subsequent work, *Lessons from History*, they conclude that a standard of morality has never existed apart from religion. In other words, the faith of a people provides the foundation for morality, and this in turn is the foundation for law and culture. Morality is the bridge between faith or theology and culture.

kingdom, and the Great Commission to make disciples who follow Christ comprise our call to globalization.

EVALUATION

In this section I wish to evaluate briefly each of these developments that give a renewed impetus to the cause of Islam in its conflict with Christianity.

Regarding the Use of the Historical-Critical Method

It is clear that Islamists have read widely in critical thinking, and use it to try to undermine the person of Christ and the content and meaning of the gospel.

Islamists appeal to scientific methodology and reason because they see nothing contradictory between the two. It was not always this way. Originally the nature of Allah as unapproachable and impenetrable meant that his creation was similarly unapproachable. A "supernatural" incentive to embrace science and reason came when Mahmun (caliph of Baghdad from 813-833) had a dream in which he saw the ghost of Aristotle, who convinced him that there is no contradiction between religion and reason.[66]

There are significant problems for Islam in her embrace of the historical-critical method. First, Islam's use of this method is inconsistent. On the one hand Islam appeals to "science" to decipher the good from the bad, at least in its traditions, yet rejects any scientific application to the Qur'an to test its text, claims, etc. It is also contradictory for Islamists to seek to destroy the authority of the Bible at certain points while yet insisting that they view the Bible as authoritative at other places, and cite it as such.

There are also great dangers in using the historical-critical method.

---

[66] Lothar Schmalfuss, "Science, Art and Culture in Islam , *Eerdmans' Handbook*, 327.

To appeal to a modern scientific worldview is inherently atheistic, naturalistic, or agnostic. While there may be a limited place for such an appeal, within certain bounds, Muslims would use it pervasively as the basis for faulting Christianity and supporting Islam.[67]

Islam is naïve in appealing to the historical-critical method. It claims to be "scientific" in its application of higher criticism and in its use of lower criticism. Yet higher criticism is not scientific, as both its proponents and opponents acknowledge. While lower criticism may be more scientific, even it can be highly subjective and reflect higher critical attitudes. Islamists have virtually no manuscript support for the readings they contest.[68]

Another problem concerns misrepresentation of the claims of the historical-critical method. Muhsin never refers to the historical-critical method in such terms. Yet he refers to the characteristics of it by appealing to science, reason, what is contrary to history, and to corrupted additions or distortions of the text of the Bible, especially in John and Paul who, he claims, make Jesus divine. He deliberately accuses Paul of later perverting the gospel of Jesus and of the apostles and being an evil doer. This reflects the historical-critical method articulated by F. C. Baur and the Tubingen school (see appendix two). What Muhsin and his critical sources don't tell the reader is that virtually all of Baur's reconstruction of early Christianity has not been confirmed by subsequent scholarship.[69] Baur's methods were often "neither critical, scientific, nor historical."[70] In charging Paul with corrupting the gospel of Christ and the Apostles, Muhsin is either deceptive or uninformed. Baur said just the opposite. He claimed that Pauline

---

[67] The historical-critical method is valid to the extent that it is a tool to discover truth in texts and in the universe around us, for God is the author of all truth. There is truth in the historical-critical method. Yet Scripture is the ultimate interpreter of all claims to truth, both Islam's and Christianity's.
[68] A crucial case in point is the claim made to substitute *periclytos* for *paracletos* (cited above). There is absolutely no manuscript support for such a reading. It is based on nothing but wishful desire for corruption of the text (John 14:26).
[69] Stephen Neill, *The Interpretation of the New Testament 1861-1961* (London: Oxford, 1966), 27, points out that the presuppositions of Baur are wrong:

It is in the field of its presuppositions, which in themselves have nothing to do with critical or historical method, that the whole great structure of the work of Baur comes to grief. Again and again, when the presuppositions are exercising their unfortunate influence, critical method is for the time being abandoned.

[70] Ibid., 25. Baur's work was marred by two great weaknesses: provincialism and special pleading (20). We should not imagine, Neill adds, that "the Christian faith as presented by Strauss or Baur is the same as the Christian faith of the Church in the earlier centuries" (32).

Christianity is "far more authoritative" than that of the Jewish party of Peter.[71]

Muhsin believes that criticism has shown that John's Gospel is unhistorical. Yet Neill points out that just the opposite is true. It is one of the "positive achievements" of New Testament study that John's Gospel "holds firmly to the historic manifestation of God in Jesus Christ; but it is primarily a theological restatement of the meaning of that manifestation."[72]

Islamists should also note that use of the historical-critical method is a two-edged sword. If Islamists are going to use it against Christianity, they are validating the value of the method. Islam then must be willing to submit to the method, and this can be devastating. The Qur'an itself has alterations and abrogations.[73] Morey documents over one hundred contradictions and errors regarding the Bible, history, science, and other matters as found in the Qur'an.[74]

The preceding suggests that Islam is not really engaged in the historical-critical method. Rather it subtly uses what it wants from the enemies of evangelical faith in order to attack Christianity and discards the rest (including the more recent findings of the historical-critical method). Suspicions regarding objectivity and fairness naturally arise when opponents of Christianity, rather than Christians themselves, claim that they know what is true in Christianity and what is not.[75]

In the end Islam should be wary of using a tool imported from Western

---

[71] Ibid., 24. Neill goes on: It is "universally agreed" that Paul's Epistles (especially 1 Thessalonians, Galatians, Romans, 1 and 2 Corinthians) give us "our earliest pictures of the Christian Church and of the Christian faith" (399). This is one of the "positive achievements" of the years 1861-1961 (338).

[72] Ibid., 340.

[73] Christy Wilson, "The Qur'an," *Eerdmans Handbook*, 315. For example, Sura 2:150 orders Muslims to pray toward Jerusalem. When the Jews failed to follow Muhammad, the direction of prayer was changed to Mecca (2:125). Such alterations are explained by Sura 2:106: "If we abrogate a verse or consign it to oblivion, we offer something better than it or something of equal value." With this approach any seeming contradiction can be avoided.

[74] Morey, *Islamic Invasion*, 137-155.

[75] Muhsin spends most of his time citing the detractors or enemies of evangelical Christianity. He does not appear to cite a single evangelical. When he cites friends of Christianity one gets the sense that he is citing them out of context. The early church father, Tertullian, noted that the best interpreters of Christianity are Christians, not its opponents. From this Christians also should learn that a better approach to evaluating Islam would be to reiterate constantly the gospel message rather than seek to expose all the faults of Islam, although there is a place for the latter.

liberal theology. It is another indication of the weakness of Christianity and may contaminate Islam. Also, Christians should not want Islam to use such a method since they do not want potential Christians among Muslims to be deceived by "deceitful philosophy" and the "traditions of men" (Col. 2:8). Christians and Muslims alike should be wary of "science" and "reason" for they may be opposed to faith and so violate a Biblical worldview (Heb. 11:1, 6).[76][77]

Finally, the rise of postmodernism has seriously challenged the very presuppositions of the historical-critical method. It challenges reason and science as the sole determiners of truth and allows for other sources of truth (revelation, experience, intuition). While postmodernism has its own problems, it points to the inadequacy of Islamists' claims based on the historical-critical method and reason.

Islam also suffers a serious handicap. It cannot appeal to the role of the Holy Spirit as the infallible guide to truth, for there is no divine Spirit in Islam. There is no divine revealer of truth (Eph. 1:17-18). When it comes to interpretation, there is no promise that the Holy Spirit will lead to truth in interpretation (John 14:26; 15:26; 1 Cor. 2:10-16). In addition,

---

[76] Neill, *Interpretation*, 28, quotes Horst Stephan as noting that Baur's approach failed to recognize in church history "the living character which it derives from the Christian belief in God." In contrast, the Cambridge Three (Lightfoot, Westcott, Hort) regarded the "key of faith" as "wholly compatible with a strictly scientific use of evidence, and in no way as a substitute for it" (88).

Neill fully embraces the historical-critical method. The "scientific and critical approach" is established and one of the "positive achievements" of New Testament study (338, 346). It is the results of the method that distinguishes liberals from conservatives (338). He asserts that the method is not the problem, but the presuppositions are (30-31). Yet he raises the central question whether the Bible is like any other book and so to be interpreted like any other book. Does inspiration make a difference? He does not believe so (30-31). Yet both Muslims and evangelicals must insist that inspiration does make a difference. In addition, postmodernism raises concerns that justify a skeptical attitude toward the higher critical method itself. Various Biblical texts make it clear that one cannot interpret the Bible correctly apart from the work of the Holy Spirit. The nature of Scripture, with its deeper meaning, and the role of the Holy Spirit affect not only presuppositions but the method of interpreting the Bible. We must be wary of a method that is based in science and reason rather than revelation.

[77] There is no clearer example of how certain professed Christians have rejected the biblical worldview than that of Rudolf Bultmann in his *New Testament and Mythology and Other Basic Writings* (Schubert M. Ogden, ed., trans. (Philadelphia: Fortress, 1984). He acknowledged that presuppositions are involved in historical-critical research (151); that the "world picture of the New Testament is a mythical world picture" (1); and that it is pointless and impossible for Christians today to acknowledge this world picture to be true because it is the world picture not informed by modern scientific thinking (3). Note above how Muhsin cited him.

there is little or no appeal to a deeper level of meaning to which Jesus, the Apostles, and early Christians appealed as derived from the divine Author who often spoke beyond the understanding of the human author. For the Qur'an, the text comes directly from God, with Muhammed being only a conveyer of God's words. There is no idea of inspiration but only dictation.[78]

The place given to Jesus Christ and his person and work is critical for Christianity and for Islam. He is the "explanation," the "interpretation," the "exegesis" of God; we cannot know God apart from him (John 1:18). To deny Christ is to lose God (2 John 9). He is the essence of deity (Rom. 9:5; Col. 2:9; Heb. 1:2-3). The contemporary politically-correct speech that downplays the differences between Islam and Christianity flounders on the different views as to who Jesus Christ is. Appendix three summarizes these differences.

The relationship of Christ to God the Father leads naturally to the other significant question: Who is Allah? Is he the God of the Bible? While God is the father of all in a general sense (Acts 17:28), ultimately he is not the God of those who reject Jesus Christ. See appendix four regarding this.

Regarding a Secular Worldview

To meet the challenge of Islam on the level of worldview is much more difficult and demanding. In some respects Muslims put Christians to shame for the latter's failure to live according to a biblical worldview and for being too heavily influenced by the secularism of the culture. The constant prayer of every devout Muslim is that Allah's will be done.

While Islam itself faces its own secularization, there is presently a revival of fundamentalism. In the face of Western power, there is a new spirit of self-confidence based in the economic power of oil and the influence associated with it. While Anderson believes that the chequered pattern of secularization, revival, and evolving adaptations in the past will be the course of the future, only time will tell.[79]

---

[78] Those who criticize evangelicals for holding to a dictation theory ought to turn their attention to Islam and its unabashed dictation (which however, rests on the claim of what Muhammad himself said Allah said).

[79] Norman Anderson, "The Future of Islam," *Eerdmans' Handbook*, 334. He wrote ten years ago and even then acknowledged that Islam and Christianity were actively competing with Marxism (now defunct) for the soul of Africa.

The historical-critical method and a secular worldview are directly related. Rudolf Bultmann and other critics assert that our modern, scientific worldview has replaced the biblical worldview with its miracles, angels, and the deity of Christ. Critical methodology makes rationalism the authority to judge revelation, and leaves people with no supernatural realm, no ultimate truth, no firm standard for moral behavior.

To the extent that Christians have bought into such a worldview they are part of the problem, not part of the solution, in meeting the challenge of Islam. It is an affront to both Islam and Christianity, and to truth itself, for secularists to gloss over the religious differences between Christianity and Islam. Secularists cast a blind eye toward deeply held beliefs that make all the difference, especially that concerning the deity of Christ.[80]

The great values of freedom, human dignity, and self-restraint under law as based in Christianity are strangely absent from the secularists' vision of our past, present, and future. They make little attempt to raise the discussion to this level because they have rejected Christianity. The worldview of secularism is natural and earth-centered, and disallows the realm of the spiritual and supernatural. It promotes materialism, naturalism, and immoral behavior—the very values the secularists attempt to denounce!—and undermines spirituality and accountability. These values transcend cultures and call for sacrifice to preserve them.[81]

Indeed, the secular view of history only validates the Muslim's

---

Woodberry, "War on Terrorism," 3-4, cites five reasons for Muslim hatred toward the West: (1) the Israel-Palestine conflict; (2) the continued sanctions against Iraq; (3) the Muslim sense of being humiliated and in danger (they see themselves with a superior culture but the West with superior power); (4) the West is corroding morality and exporting it; and (5) Americans with their superior power talked about democracy but did not back it up when it did not serve their purposes, as in Algeria. See also Nabeel Jabbour's book, *The Rumbling Volcano*, which deals with fundamentalism in Egypt.

[80] For example, one's view of the person of Jesus Christ has significant consequences. Christians believe Jesus to be God incarnate while Muslims reject his deity. The difference is strategic and crucial. For one thing, it is Jesus who set forth the ethic of love. In the Sermon on the Mount he taught his followers to "love their enemies as they love themselves." Because he is God Christians are compelled to follow Jesus, to live in peace with their opponents. Because Muslims are not disciples of Christ they are not similarly compelled. Is it any wonder that Islam rejects or neglects his ethic of love toward enemies?

[81] Just a few days after the attack on America, on September 20, 2001, President Bush spoke to the nation and to the world about the importance of such values and the faith upon which they rest. He noted that the war on terrorism is about values such as freedom, justice, and democracy. God,

complaint against the West—that we are a secular society that has lost its spiritual moorings and bred all sorts of evil. In other words, the secular view, rather than providing a solution to the problem, only exacerbates it. By its reductionistic argument that the "root cause" of Muslim anger is US foreign policy this view reveals the very decadence Muslims fault us for—failing to recognize the deepest claims of religious faith. A defective foreign policy does not constitute a *root cause* but the *effect* of something else—a secular worldview. It is this that is a root cause, and secularists promote it.

Most alarmingly, the secularists deprive the West of the only thing able to win in the clash of civilizations—a superior moral position based in love, faith, and truth. By their misunderstanding and avoidance of the crucial role of religion to transform our culture, including our foreign policy, they invite realization of the very thing they hope will not come, the clash of civilizations, and our incapacity to meet it.[82]

The conflict with Islam is a spiritual one, involving forces and powers of a spiritual nature. It is not with flesh and blood. Hence our methods for confronting such opponents must be based in spiritual values. Paul clearly spells out the Christian's methods for engagement in Ephesians 6:10-20.

Since Islam embraces both Testaments, Christians must properly

---

he said, is not neutral in the conflict between freedom and fear, justice and cruelty. The terrorists who do evil in the name of Allah have blasphemed the name of Allah.

These great values sprang from the Christian West, not from the East or the Muslim world. Wherever *sharia*, or Islamic law, is instituted, there is no democracy or personal freedom on a par with what people enjoy in the US or West. *Sharia* accompanies totalitarianism. Along with many other freedoms, our most basic freedom, the freedom of religion, would be denied or severely restricted. Contemporary news from Nigeria, Sudan, Israel, and Indonesia makes this all too clear.

The differences between the Christian West and the Muslim world derive from fundamental values that transformed a barbaric West in the 4th century when Constantine became a Christian. The founding fathers of our nation embraced these values as universal, and it is this universality that has given them their great appeal.

[82] A clash of civilizations has a precedent in history. In the 5th century, decadent Christian Rome, while militarily superior to all others, fell to pagan invaders.

In the present conflict there is one basis for optimism, but it is not found where the secularists think. It is found in transcendent, spiritual values. It is they that have the power to transform our culture, and even Islam, along more just, generous, and beneficial lines.

If an apocalyptic clash of civilizations comes, it will do so not because of US foreign policy but because of a secular worldview that has rejected Christian values of dignity, truth, and spirituality. These derive from a divine presence in the universe.

understand the place of the Old Testament in their belief system. If Christians are to have and understand a biblical worldview they must practice the worldview found within Scripture. It is the worldview that the New Testament reinforces from the Old Testament.[83]

What about the values of honor and avoidance of shame? While Islam often treasures values (as discussed above) that are often more in line with Scripture than what our Western culture embraces, not all of these values should have the place that Islam and Middle East culture give them. The values of honor and respect are to be highly prized, and Scripture treasures these as well.[84] Yet embracing the truth no matter what the consequences and sacrificing all for Christ's sake are greater values than personal honor and saving face.[85] Muslim attachment to the values of honor and avoidance of shame can be just as idolatrous as our culture's attachment to materialism and pleasure. This attachment helps us to understand why it is extremely difficult to get to the truth in conflicts with Muslims.

Conflicting values represented by Christianity and Islam suggest that it is appropriate to ask: What is it about Islam that encourages world conquest and totalitarianism? Is it not its view of Allah? Its view of the nature of human beings and sin? Its view of the nature of government and

---

[83] A proper understanding of the relationship between the Testaments is basic to all Christian theology—regarding the nature of God, Christ, the Spirit, Scripture. It is basic to an effective response to Islam which bases so much of its beliefs on the Old Testament and its relationship to the New. Christian instruction must give thorough treatment to the Bible and its interpretation, and wrestle with the significant issues of the believer's relationship to the law, the means of salvation and redemption, the role of faith, and the future of the believer (the resurrection of the body, the kingdom, and other matters of eschatology).

[84] Over 600 passages mention honor, shame, or disgrace. For example, humanity is "crowned with glory and honor" (Psalm 8), and the Fifth Commandment tells us to "honor" our parents. Paul exhorts Christians to honor those deserving such (Rom. 13:7), to honor others above themselves (Rom. 12:10), including double honor for elders (1 Tim. 5:17). He often cites shame as the reason to order community life in a certain way (1 Cor. 11; 14:34, 40). Yet these values have limits. The Ninth Commandment prohibits lying. Hence we are to honor parents, and respect family values, but not at the expense of the truth.

[85] Jesus was willing to fulfill God's purpose, to die on behalf of sinful humanity, even if this meant terrible shame and dishonor (Gal. 3:13—he became a curse for us). He despised the shame (Heb. 12:2). By suffering a shameful death he is crowned with glory and honor (Heb. 2:7). Christ calls us to join him outside the camp, bearing the disgrace he bore (Heb. 13:13). Likewise, Paul warns believers to avoid what is shameful (Eph. 5:12), but he was willing to bear shame and disgrace for the sake of the gospel, to make Christ known (Phil. 3:7-8), as Peter and other apostles rejoiced to be counted worthy to suffer shame for Christ (Acts 5:41). As Jesus laid down his life for us we ought to do the same for one another (1 John 3:16).

civilization?[86]

There is a qualification to the concern that Christians need to renounce a secular worldview. As pilgrims in a foreign land they do not want to force their culture in the direction of dominion theology or a theocracy. This would violate the attribute of freedom in human nature. The attendant political freedom allows Christianity (and other religions) to flourish. As Victor Davis Hanson asserts, a "secular rationalism" is part of the American system that will often invite hate from others and have to be defended, even by going to war.[87] It is in this culture that Christianity is given its greatest opportunity and need not feel threatened as freedom is extended to all. Christians know the truth, and the freedom that accompanies it (cf. 1 John 5:20; John 8:32; cf. 14:6).

There is a delicate balance that needs to be maintained, as our founding fathers themselves framed it. Our freedoms need to be exercised with a moral restraint, but we cannot force upon our society the religion or faith that provides the basis for this morality. To do so will entail the use of secular means to secure spiritual objectives (rejected in Scripture: Zech. 4:6). Our society simply needs to reinforce the great affirmations of our founding documents that witness to a biblical worldview of reality: God has created all people, and he is the source of all our rights (so state the Declaration of Independence and the U.S. Constitution). These affirmations embrace the realm of the spiritual in the most basic way. Yet the First Amendment prohibits a national church while allowing unrestricted freedom of religion.

This balance is anchored to the teaching of Jesus who implicitly elevates the place of the secular state. He exhorted his detractors to give proper allegiance to the state and proper allegiance to God (Matt. 22:15-22). This at once prohibits a theocracy and secularism. Paul and Peter reinforce the same message when they exhort limited allegiance to the (secular)

---

[86] Nationhood is a biblical concept and part of God's plan for the world (cf. Gen. 10-11). To unite the world under one system (fascism, communism, or Islam) will bring greater evil than what individual states can muster. In seeking to form a brotherhood that exceeds national and ethnic identities, that forces all to live under *sharia*, Islam opposes the biblical pattern exemplified by Christ as the pattern for this age.

[87] Victor Davis Hanson, "Classics and War," abridged version of a lecture at a seminar on "Liberal Education, Liberty, and Education Today" given at Hillsdale College, November 11, 2001, and printed in *Imprimis*, February 2002 (31:2) 1-5.

state as ordained by God (Rom. 13:1-7), to "fear God and honor the king" (1 Pet. 2:13-17).

On the other hand, the state is to enact law that promotes public morality (1 Tim. 1:8-10), godliness and human dignity (1 Tim. 2:1-2), Paul asserts. It is destructive to allow freedom to become license for the very practices that seek to secularize our state to the exclusion of religion from all public recognition. These practices would turn it from the Christian values regarding the nature of human beings that brought us such freedoms in the first place.

The feared clash of civilizations is really a clash of worldviews. The worldviews of Christianity and Islam are at odds, and the worldview of secularism is bankrupt in trying to assess the nature of the collision.

Regarding Globalization

Islam has its own vision of globalization, and it is not primarily, not even secondarily, economic. It is first of all religious or spiritual.[88] The drive of Islam is to establish a worldwide community, a brotherhood, where Allah is worshipped. Yet the means to do this are under serious scrutiny and debate, even within Islam. The Qur'an supports both a peaceful way (Sura 2:256: "Let there be no compulsion in religion") and a brutal way (Sura 5:33: "The punishment of those who wage war against God and His Messenger . . . is: execution, or crucifixion, or cutting off of hands and feet . . . .").[89]

Jihad has both a spiritual and a military meaning.[90] Beverley believes that the greatest clash today in the world is not between Islam and the West but "the clash between Muslims as they try to define their faith for

---

[88] Rarely do leaders in the West acknowledge this spiritual dimension. President Bush is an apparent, refreshing exception (note his speech to the nation and to the world on 9-20-01). Yet even he does not speak openly enough about the exportation of Christian spiritual values. His speaking about Islam as a "religion of peace" undermines this opportunity.

[89] Other passages exist that call Muslims to fight. "Fighting is prescribed for you" (Sura 2:216); "Fight in the cause of God those who fight you and slay them for tumult and oppression are worse than slaughter. Fight them until there is no more persecution and oppression and there prevails justice and faith in God" (2:190-192); "Fight and slay the infidels" (9:5); and "The true believers are those who strive with their lives for the cause of God" (49:15).

[90] Jabbour, in his remarks at World View Center (see above), notes that *jihad* has three meanings. It is striving against sin in one's life and striving to follow God; striving to lead others to do likewise; and using physical means to force Islam on others (when the first two actions fail).

the 21st century."[91]

Christianity can take encouragement from the fact that it has been the major stimulus to a form of political system that has become the envy of the world.[92]

Yet Christianity's greatest impact has been its moral and spiritual influence, for this is what lies behind all its other contributions. It is just here that its influence is being perverted within and this corruption is what is also being exported abroad.

Modern Islam contrasts the contributions of Christianity. The global designs of Islam are often accompanied by economic, cultural, and political breakdown, and little freedom exists.[93]

Christianity, not Islam, is in a unique position to shape the course of the world (so Matt. 5:13-16). Only Christianity is the truly global faith. Only Christianity can be indigenous. Only Christianity with its high view of the nature of people can bequeath those values of human freedom and dignity to globalization and democracy to keep them from becoming destructive. Only Christianity maintains the proper balance between the state and the church, between personal sovereignty and divine sovereignty. Only Christianity is adaptable to indigenous peoples. Only Christianity affirms the truth that is able to make one free (John 8:32).

The issue of globalization is tied closely to the other concerns of this paper. On the basis of historical-critical methodology Islamists assert that Jesus never commissioned his followers to go to all the world. It is only Muhammad who was given a universal message to unite all the world in submission to Allah. Islam is impelled by a heavenly mindset or worldview that refuses to divorce the sacred from the secular.

Does globalization work to the advantage of Christianity or Islam or both? It can do so for both. The point is that globalization cannot be

---

[91] James A. Beverley, "Is Islam a Religion of Peace?" *Christianity Today* (January 7, 2002) 38. In this very fine article Beverley lays out three answers to his question, and decides that the answer is yet unknown. It is the central debate within Islam. Beverley's article also provides what he calls the "best resources on Islam" (36).

[92] Future historians, no doubt, will affirm that America's influence has been at least as great as, if not greater than, that of ancient Egypt, Greece, and Rome. It has brought more freedom to more people than any other force in history.

[93] Beverley, "Islam," 40, points out that of the 41 countries that are at least 70 percent Muslim, 26 are considered not free by the United Nations Declaration of Human Rights, 13 are partially free, and only two are free. See also the statistics cited earlier in the section, "The Role of Globalization."

avoided. The earlier discussion regarding globalization pointed out the essential relationship between freedom and religion. In this area Christianity has the advantage over Islam. Islam's geographical, linguistic, and cultural centers act as barriers to universalism. Evangelical faith is superior here, not only with regard to Islam but also with regard to Judaism (it has Jerusalem), and Roman Catholicism (it has its Pope and Rome). Evangelicals "do not have here a continuing city but seek the coming one," the new Jerusalem (Heb. 13:14; 12:22ff.).

There will be increasing contact between the West and the non-West, and Christians should be prepared as never before for the engagement. Theirs is the advantage.

CONCLUSION

None of the three developments that I have cited existed prior to modern times. While the cross and the crescent have always been in conflict, the rise of the modern historical-critical method, the increasing impact of a secular worldview, and globalization raise the conflict to new heights. The outcome of the conflict is uncertain. Only evangelical faith can rise to the occasion to bring clarity, understanding, and resolution to the doctrinal, worldview, and global aspects of the conflict. It must totally engage the head, the heart, and the will in the struggle. If it does not do so, then the West will be corrupted and doomed to a losing battle. For it will have surrendered the very means of its own success or victory.

What can be done in light of each of these challenges? There needs to be a realignment of evangelical mission outreaches to concentrate on the more than one billion Muslims in the world. An international gathering should work on the agenda. With presently one percent of evangelical giving going to reaching the Muslim world, funding needs to be radically altered.

In churches, Bible colleges and seminaries, there needs to be informed, serious teaching about Islam. There must be a renewed concentration on the teaching of biblical introduction, where the issues flowing from the historical-critical method (such as source, form, redaction, and reader response criticisms, structuralism, deconstruction, etc., and textual criticism) are vigorously critiqued, and, where necessary, refuted.

There must be vigorous teaching of the person and work of Christ and the nature of the trinity. Christology and the nature of God are central to the theological differences between Christianity and Islam.

There must be the urgent pursuit of the role of worldview in shaping our general approach to the Bible. Interpretation of the Bible must recognize the limitations of the approach of science, history, and grammar. It must embrace that approach which recognizes the nature of Scripture as unlike any other book.[94] It will view the text as a living oracle inspired by the Holy Spirit and will recognize that interpretation is also by the Spirit to Spirit filled people. Such a creative approach agrees with a biblical worldview.[95] A proper understanding and commitment here will forestall the challenges of the historical-critical method, secularism, and the evil aspects of globalization.

The only way to implement a mentality where the spiritual realm is fully embraced is through spiritual formation. Spiritual renewal and transformation is the need of the Church. A living, vital, interpersonal, reciprocal relationship with the triune God and his living word practiced in full consciousness of dwelling in a trinitarian universe is the only truly

---

[94] Contrary to Neill, *Interpretation*, 30. He asserts that by 1860 historical criticism had come to stay, and that "henceforward the Bible would be treated like any other book. No holds would be barred." The Scriptures had to be able "on their own merits to stand up to the challenge" or the cause of Christianity might "be held to be lost in advance."

A hermeneutic flowing from a biblical worldview will embrace the Bible's own hermeneutic and practice it. It will reject strongly those aspects of our modern hermeneutic that are contrary to it because they arise from a modern, secular, scientific mind set. The Bible views itself as special revelation of unseen reality, as unlike any other book. Thus we must interpret Scripture not as any other book. To refuse to reform our hermeneutic will increasingly leave the Bible for specialists rather than for all, and to impoverish and deprive the Church of all the creative interpretation waiting to be discovered by the Holy Spirit's empowerment.

[95] A creative hermeneutic is what the early Christians practiced, following the example of Christ himself, when they discovered Jesus Christ to be the promised Messiah. They found a level of meaning in the text that transcended the literal (or grammatical-historical) sense. The Book of Hebrews demonstrates this hermeneutic most convincingly. The approach transcended the practice of the rabbis and Pharisees, and it rejected the contemporary secular worldview represented by Plato, Philo, and others. The approach embraced the worldview of the Old Testament and its hermeneutic.

Thomas Schmidt, *A Scandalous Beauty: The Artistry of God and the Way of the Cross* (Grand Rapids: Brazos Press, 2002), 51, writes that if "we could go back in time and set up a formal debate between Jesus and a leading Pharisee of the day like Gamaliel or his student Saul, using the tools of interpretation that we would use today to interpret the relevant documents, *the Pharisee would win* (italics his)." Also Stephen Motyer, "The Psalm Quotations of Hebrews 1: A Hermeneutic-free Zone?" *Tyn Bull* 50.1 (1999) 3-22, argues that the Old Testament quotations of Hebrews 1 pose a serious challenge to an evangelical hermeneutic. He proposes a version of typology as the guiding hermeneutic, a form of the Rabbinic *gezerah shawah* (verbal analogy) principle, and argues that it is perfectly acceptable today and that we can extend it further.

Christian approach.[96] Thereby we become apprentices, disciples, of Christ.

In the West and the non-West there must come a resurgence of vital, Spirit-filled evangelical faith that embraces fully a biblical worldview. It must include a return to the reading of the Bible, a vigorous defense of its reliability, and to a hermeneutic that flows from a biblical worldview as the foundation for doing biblical and systematic theology and for moral behavior.

What does the present situation portend? Certainly the rise and growth of Islam is one of the aspects belonging to "Babylon" as portrayed in the Book of the Revelation (chapters 17-18). There Babylon represents both worldwide religion and power, economic and political, that will consume the earth in the last days prior to the return of Christ. The West, if she abandons her faith and embraces a secular view of science, the world, and globalism now pressing upon her, will also become one with Babylon.

It is, and will be, a measure of our faith that we believe that Jesus Christ is all that he claimed to be, and demonstrated, if we take him to the whole world. Will the future see Christianity supplanting the place of Islam as the world's fastest growing religion?

In the words of Hebrews, our present day and year represent another instance of the "today" available to us to turn from our unbelief (Heb. 3:7-4:11) and compromise. Will we seize the moment, to provoke love and good works, to exhort one another even more as we see the "day" approaching (Heb. 10:24-25)?

---

[96] For gaining an understanding of and appreciation for a biblical worldview I recommend, Dallas Willard, *The Divine Conspiracy: Rediscovering Our Hidden Life in God* (San Francisco: HarperSanFrancisco, 1998).

PART THREE

APPENDICES

APPENDIX ONE
THE MUSLIM MINDSET

The following quotation comes from the preface (pp. 3-5) of Ali Muhsin's *Let the Bible Speak*. The spelling or grammatical peculiarities in the following quotation are Muhsin's.

The writing and publication of this essay is not intended to be an exercise in polemics. Rather is it motivated by the desire to enlighten both Christians and Muslims who in many parts of the world have to live together as fellow countrymen and neighbors. Their enlightenment regarding the original fundamentals of each other's faith would, it is hoped, make them appreciate the basic unity that binds them as adherents of the same original faith, the Universal Religion which teaches submission to the will of the one True God as the basis on which man's moral behavior is founded.

It is unfortunate that Jesus Christ has left for us nothing as authoritative as the Prophet Muhammad has done. In the Qur'an are the teaching of Islam in their unsullied purity. We do not find the same in the Gospels (Injeel). The latter may be compared to the traditions of the Prophet (the Hadiths or Sunna). Of the sayings and actions of Jesus as reported in the Bible there are admittedly many which are spurious, false, just as there were established and the weak and false were weeded out. It is undeniable that attempts were made, for sectarian and other divisive reasons, to fake sayings and attribute them to the Prophet.

Impartial criticism would have to admit, however, that there was much more scientific methodology when the Prophet's traditions came to be collected and shifted than there has been at the adoption of the canonical Gospels. The great scholars (Imams) who devoted their lives collecting the traditions of the Prophet made their best endeavors (Ijtihad) using strictly scientific standards to verify the genuine traditions. But even their best endeavors and their scientific methods were after all human and not infallible. Fortunately there is the Qur'an whose authenticity has never been questioned by friend or foe. That is the unshakable foundation of Islam on which the tenets of the faith are based. It is the final criterion of the genuineness of any tradition, and the rock on which the structure of Islam has been built.

•   •   •   •   •

I would appeal to both my Muslim brothers and sisters who know very little of Christianity, and to my Christian friends who know next to nothing about true Islam (and true Christianity for that matter) to come along with me, and in the following pages search for the truth. We will find it, for the truth is the house that has been founded upon the Rock, and rain shall fall, and the winds shall blow, but the house shall not fall. There in Holy Jerusalem whence both Muhammad and Jesus rose in spiritual ecstasy to the Heavenly Presence is a symbol of glaring significance, denoting the truth that bids both Muslim and Christian bow to the same God who is worshipped with equal fervor and devotion in the Mosque upon the Rock and in the Church of the Holy Sepulchre. That Truth bids us rid ourselves of the traditions of men and follow the commandments of God. That Truth bids us relinquish the tendency to divide Religion into sects and uphold the Unity that binds us together.

APPENDIX TWO
CRITIQUE OF THE HISTORICAL-CRITICAL METHOD

For this material summarizing the rise and influence, and subsequent failure, of the historical-critical method, I follow Gerald Bray, *Biblical Interpretation: Past and Present* (Downer's Grove: InterVarsity, 1996), 221-263; 321-368; and Stephen Neill, *The Interpretation of the New Testament 1861-1961* (London: Oxford, 1966), 19-32, 336-348.

The beginnings of higher criticism are traced back to the rise of the historical-critical method in the mid 1650's, which fought for influence for the next 200 years. By 1850 it became established in Germany, and by 1890 in England. By 1945 the method had triumphed and become the general consensus of the academic world. Since about 1970 it has begun to be questioned, and in light of the rise of postmodernism, it has serious faults.

The historical criticism of the Bible began with the "age of reason," usually dated about 1650. In England reason contested with piety and religious nonconformists. Elsewhere the intellectual diversity of Germany allowed it to begin dominating the scholarly world by 1800. During this time the study of Scripture was tied to the development of Western philosophy. Whereas reason and Scripture were at first believed to be in harmony, because God was the author of both, reason came to be used as a tool to investigate on the basis of science the truth claims of Scripture including miracles. The rationalists came to view these as irrational, and denied the deity of Christ and his resurrection, ascension, etc. In this climate other discrepancies of the Bible came to be investigated in a scientific way and greater skepticism arose. The rationalists felt that religion and the Bible had to be purified of irrational and immoral elements—a process that Jesus and Paul began but failed and that the rationalists felt they had to complete.

Yet there always were those who resisted such rationalism. Toward the end of the eighteenth century a new current of romanticism, similar to today's evangelicalism, arose whose followers believed that the Bible could not be reduced to a historical document and that something deeper was involved which rationalism missed. Also neologists believed that the Bible should be read in a fundamentally new way. While they used the critical method they were more receptive to miracles and other supernatural elements of Scripture. Thus neology divorced exegesis from theology. This position came to dominate nineteenth-century biblical interpretation.

During the nineteenth century the rationalist approach to the Bible evolved into a rewriting of early church history so that the New Testament itself was viewed as witnessing to three competing circles of influence. This view of F. C. Baur and the "Tubingen school of interpretation" identified the circles as Palestinian Judaism (represented by Jesus), Diaspora Judaism (represented by Paul), and Hellenistic Gentiles. With the fall of Jerusalem in A. D. 70, the former groups merged with the last one to form a new church. Under persecution and heavily influenced by Greek philosophy this church hardened its theology and resisted heresy in the forms of an imminent "parousia hope" and gnosticism. Jesus came to be viewed as a moderately successful rabbi who had internalized the moral demands of the law. Opposition to this led to his death. Baur's reconstruction of Christianity followed Hegel's philosophy that Christianity is a new synthesis developed from an early thesis (Judaism) and antithesis (Hellenism).

Yet in 1906 the appearance of Albert Schweitzer's *The Quest for the Historical Jesus* showed that Jesus was a far different figure—an apocalyptic, fanatical figure who expected the imminent end of the world. This led to a whole new era of research.

Baur heavily influenced twentieth-century scholarship. Paul is viewed as the champion of the Gentile party, whereas Peter represents the Judaizers. These conflicts resulted in the new synthesis of "early Catholicism" in the mid second century. The Synoptic Gospels, James, Jude, and Revelation witness to Jewish Christianity and a purely human Messiah. John, a later development of Christianity, has no value as a historical source for the life of Jesus.

While Baur has continued to have significant influence, his approach has been shown to go beyond the available evidence. For example, there is little evidence that there were two conflicting parties within early Christianity that were divided as sharply as Baur made them to be. Also scholars have shown that Paul's world was that of the rabbis not that of the Greeks. Finally, the Hellenization of the Church took place much later, in the second century (see other problems with Baur's approach in Bray, 359-61).

However, some Muslims, such as Muhsin, rely heavily on the approach of Baur.

Muhsin has also been highly influenced by the "history of religions" approach. This affirms that Christianity is a syncretism of other religions with Judaism. Arising in the late nineteenth and early twentieth centuries, this approach makes Christianity like other religions of the era. Foreign, oriental religions and their mythology were combined with Greek mystery religions and Judaism to produce Christianity, at least as represented in Paul and John (see Bray, 361-366). Yet Schweitzer's work, in which he viewed Christianity as arising wholly within Jewish apocalyptic apart from any Greek influence, demolishes this approach.

APPENDIX THREE
CONTRASTS BETWEEN JESUS AND MUHAMMAD

The following chart shows the differences between Jesus and Muhammad as viewed by Christianity. These points are derived from the Qur'an only, before later myths were concocted to make parallels to Jesus, as Morey points out.[97] The contrasts are from Morey, with slight changes.

Jesus	Muhammad
Prophesied by OT	Prophesied by neither soothsayers, the OT nor the NT
Miraculous virgin birth	Ordinary birth
Sinless (2 Cor. 5:21)	Sinful (Sura 18:110; 40:55; 48:1-2)
Did miracles	No miracles (later made up for him)
Preached the love of God	Did not preach the love of God
Both divine and human	Only human
Greatest teacher ever	Ecstatic, confused speeches
High moral example	Killed, robbed, coerced, directed others to do so
Abrogated dietary laws	Kept prohibitions of pork and wine
No child sexual involvement	Married an eight-year old (as was customary)
Died for others' sins	Died for his own sins
Rose from the dead	Died and remains dead
Ascended to heaven	Did not ascend

---

[97] Morey, *Islamic Invasion*, 89-104.

Interceding in heaven	Not he nor any other is an intercessor (Sura 6:51, 70, 10:3)
Worshipped as Savior	Not worshipped—only a man
Personal relationship to his own	No personal relationship—he's dead!
Will return to earth to judge	Will not return nor judge anyone

APPENDIX FOUR
CONTRASTS BETWEEN THE ALLAH OF THE QUR'AN AND THE GOD OF THE BIBLE

In comparing Allah as revealed in the Qur'an with the God as revealed in Scripture, Morey points out several differences that make it clear that they are not worshipped as one and the same. The Allah of the Qur'an is the God of the Bible, but he is not recognized.

(1) The attributes of Allah contrast those of the God of the Bible.[98]

    a. Unknowable versus knowable.

    b. Nonpersonal versus personal.

    c. Nonspiritual versus spiritual.

    d. Unitarian versus trinitarian.

    e. Unlimited versus limited (God is limited by his nature).

    f. Capricious versus trustworthy.

    g. No love of God versus love of God.[99]

    h. Passive versus active in history.

    i. No attributes versus attributes. (Allah's 99 are all negative—what he is not).

    j. Works versus grace.

---

[98] Ibid., 57-65.

[99] According to the remarks of Nabeel Jabbour (see the note above), there is no unconditional love associated with Allah. Allah is love, but he loves those who love him. There is no address of Allah as father, since he is unknowable.

It seems that one could say more. Since "God is love" (1 John 4:8, 19) there must be some way in which God expressed his love for all eternity. He did so within the trinity. Since Allah is not part of a trinity, there is no way for him to express this love prior to creation. This is a serious shortcoming of Islam.

(2) The monotheism of Islam does not make Allah the God of the Bible.

    a. "Allah" was the name of a pagan deity which Muhammad elevated to the "only" God.

    b. The biblical authors "would never have confused Allah with Jehovah any more than they would have confused Ba'al with Jehovah" (Morey, 64).

    c. When the Arabic Bible was translated in the ninth century, it used "Allah" to translate "God" because it was the common name for him as a result of the dominance of Islam.